Anise

Borage

Catnip

Lovage

Fennel

Sage

Sorrel

Sesame

Tarragon

Garlic

Rue

Lemon
Verbena

Poppy

THE TASTING SPOON

Loris Troup

THE
TASTING
SPOON

*How to use over 130 spices, herbs,
condiments, flavorings, to enhance all
your dishes and add zest to any menu.*

The Citadel Press   •   New York

Dedicated to

MISS WILMA

The author and the publisher wish to express their grateful appreciation for the cooperation and assistance kindly offered by DURKEE FAMOUS FOODS.

The contents of *The Tasting Spoon* have been checked for accuracy and authenticity by DURKEE FAMOUS FOODS, whose knowledge has added greatly to the completeness of this volume. We thank them also for the source material for the illustrated end papers.

LORIS TROUP
THE CITADEL PRESS

Contents

FOREWORD

The Tasting Spoon offers the spicy "secrets" of a great number of good cooks—from the cook-friends of my childhood to the one who only recently urged, "Just *try* Cardamom Seed in Apple Pie!" (Good.) My sincere thanks go to all the friends who have given freely of their culinary knowledge.

Much of the information has come, of course, from the pleasant hours spent in my own kitchen, for cooking is my hobby. But if cooking is my hobby, seasonings are my fascination, for I learned early that they can be any cook's open sesame to a whole kitchenful of adventures, but that—most important—seasonings can make simple food memorable.

L. T.

You will find the Seasoning Chart at the end of the book a helpful cross-reference; pick your dish and you can readily see which seasonings might be effectively used with it. The seasonings themselves have been arranged alphabetically in the body of the book.

Introduction

There's no mystery to using seasoning. They aren't even complicated. And without savory seasoning even the most artistic culinary creation will fall on its face.

THE COOK'S BEST RULE . . .

Season to Taste, that vague yet realistic rule, is still fundamental to the preparation of good food. However, a little more specific information can save hours of experimenting and any number of food flops for those cooks, young and old, who haven't given much thought to seasonings.

Because people's likes and dislikes vary widely in food flavors as in everything else—and the flavors of seasonings themselves vary, especially if the seasonings are not properly stored—there are few authorities on seasonings. And were there a great number of authorities, each cook would still be a rule unto herself, for through the use of seasonings she is trying to achieve only one thing: flavor combinations that are pleasing to her and her family.

It is true, of course, that rules don't necessarily make good cooks, for fifteen different cooks may begin with the same recipe and still turn out fifteen different products. Some results will be inferior, others average, but one or two may be superior to the original recipe itself, because those cooks used seasonings more imaginatively than the printed recipe suggested. (Had the cooks altered the flour or the eggs very likely the chemistry of cooking would have been upset, but changing quantities of seasonings called for has no effect on the chemical balance of a recipe.)

In improving on the original recipe the cooks followed no rules other than that old admonition *Season to Taste.*

Although it may take a little experience before the young

cook feels brave enough to alter a recipe, every cook, sooner or later, learns that she can often improve published recipes by varying the suggested seasonings.

WHAT ARE SEASONINGS?

The term *Spices* is often used broadly to include all seasonings, but a little clearer understanding of a few basic seasoning terms can quickly dispel any confusion that may now surround them:

Spices come from the bark, roots, leaves, stems, buds, seeds, or fruit of aromatic plants and trees which usually grow only in tropical countries. Pepper, Allspice, Cloves, Nutmeg, Mace, Cinnamon, Ginger, Saffron, and Turmeric are Spices. Most Spices are available either whole or ground; they are always dried.

Herbs are soft, succulent plants which usually grow in the temperate zone and, like Spices, are adaptable for flavoring, seasoning, or coloring foods. Oregano, Chervil, Marjoram, Mint, Basil, Parsley, Rosemary, Sage, Savory, Tarragon, Thyme, and Bay Leaf are Herbs. (Although Bay Leaf comes from a large tree this seasoning is popularly classed as an "herb.") Herbs may be used fresh or dried; most are available whole or ground, and some in crushed form.

Blends of Spices and Herbs are often used in cookery. Some of the most popular ones are Apple Pie Spice, Poultry Seasoning, Chili Powder, Curry Powder, Pumpkin Pie Spice, Mincemeat Spice, Flavor Salt, and Pickling Spice. The formula for a Blend may vary with the spice packer.

Spices and Herbs are classified in many different ways, but some of the most frequently used terms are these:

Aromatic Spices are those that have an especially pronounced, fragrant flavor, such as Anise, Caraway, Cardamom, Cinnamon, Cloves, Cumin, Ginger, Mace, Nutmeg, and Fennel.

Stimulating Spices include those that have an especially zesty, pungent flavor, such as Pepper, Turmeric, and Mustard.

Sweet Herbs are those plants whose leaves, stems, or roots have an aroma or flavor that makes them adaptable to cookery. Thyme, Mint, Basil, Fennel, Marjoram, Sage, and Savory are among the Sweet Herbs.

Salad Herbs are those plants we use to season salads; they include the Sweet Herbs.

Pot Herbs are not seasonings; they are food plants such as cabbage and spinach.

Fine Herbs (Fines herbes) means a combination of minced Herbs used to season such things as Soups, Steaks, Omelets, Sauces, Green Salads, and Creamed Egg or Cheese Dishes; the minced Herbs remain a part of the food. A Fine Herb combination may vary with the cook but might include Parsley, Chives, and Chervil; or Burnet, Parsley, and Thyme; or Chives, Basil, and Parsley. At one time Tarragon was popular in Fine Herbs, but since its flavor tends to dominate the Herb slipped from grace for this particular use.

Bouquet usually refers to sprigs of Herbs tied together in a "bouquet" for ease of removal from cooked food before it is served.

Seeds come from both Spices and Herbs, so, of course, some come from the tropical zone and others from the temperate zone. Some of the savory seeds that are used in preparing fine food are Anise, Cardamom, Coriander, Caraway, Mustard, Celery, Dill, Cumin, Fennel, Fenugreek, Poppy, and Sesame. Although America grows some aromatic seeds, a large quantity is imported from Africa, Europe, and South and Central America.

Flavorings and *Extracts* are the bottled essence of Spices, Herbs, Fruits, Nuts, Liqueurs, etc., which is usually preserved in an alcohol base. (Incidentally, a sweet food is usually said to be "flavored," a nonsweet one to be "seasoned.")

Vegetable Seasonings are distinctively-flavored vegetables such as Garlic, Leek, and Onion which may be served as a food or used as a seasoning in other foods. These plants are often called "herbs" when used as seasonings.

Condiments are usually liquid or semi-liquid combinations of seasonings, although we often use the word broadly (like "spices") to include all seasonings. True Condiments are such things as Tabasco, Worcestershire and other sauces; Catsup; Prepared Mustared, etc. (Relishes which are served to accompany meats are also sometimes called Condiments.)

A few seasonings are *Chemicals;* among these are Monosodium Glutamate and Salt. (An Herb-flavored Salt is often called a "condiment.")

Still other ingredients, some of which are also foods in themselves, are used to season foods: Salt Pork, Chicken Stock and Chicken Fat, Butter, Meat Drippings, Lemons, Mushrooms, Vinegars, Truffles, Wines, etc.

Have you noticed that all seasonings are nature's own products? Is it not logical to combine them with some of her other products —our foods—for more interesting taste experiences? Variety *is* the spice of cookery. In addition to flavoring food, seasonings also add color, aroma, texture contrast, and vitamins.

If your spice shelf is stocked with a few of the various types of seasonings, that's a sure sign *your* cooking isn't in a rut. In fact, an active spice shelf identifies the imaginative cook who takes pride in avoiding monotonous meals.

ONCE ONLY ROYALTY COULD ENJOY SPICES . . .

Today we take for granted Black Pepper and the other spices over which wars were once fought and in which rich ransoms were once paid. But at one time only kings and other wealthy people could afford such a delicacy as Cinnamon. Tithes were paid in Mint, Anise, and Cumin in ancient days. And four thousand years ago, rulers exchanged gifts of spices. During the Middle Ages rents were often required to be paid in precious Peppercorns. For centuries spices have been important in the rituals of many churches. Even America's discovery might have been delayed had Columbus not been salesman enough to convince his royal sponsors he might find spices on his voyage. (He was jailed because he failed to find them.)

Men braved the unknown seas, the dangers of the jungle, and the heat of the desert in their search for Nutmeg and Mace and the other tantalizing spices that then meant great wealth to the finders.

No history is richer in trickery and intrigue, prestige, greed, wealth, danger, suffering, and death than that of those innocent-looking little jars and cans of spices that sit on our kitchen cabinet shelves.

Although spices have been prized throughout the ages for their ability to make food flavors sing, in Colonial days when spices were difficult, if not impossible, to get, their use faded from American kitchens. The use of some herbs continued, however, for many had been transplated to the eastern shore of our country. However, in time, even herbs slipped from popular culinary use.

Although most foreign cookery had always excelled in using subtle, savory seasonings, it took the monotonous meals of World War II to remind us as a nation of the magic of seasonings. But just as our interest was awakened the most precious of the spices disappeared. (Remember those disappointing substitutes for Black Pepper?) However, when the war ended and the spices returned, our interest was still alive. Now, today, we have such a keen appreciation of seasonings our country is the world's largest spice buyer. (One spice company alone estimates over two million women own its spice sets.)

PLEASE THE PALATE . . .

Not even the hale and hearty relish unseasoned food, but it is even more important that the food for dieters be interestingly seasoned. The aroma and flavor of well-seasoned foods actually aid digestion, for their mouth-watering goodness literally starts the digestive juices to flowing. And everyone finds it easier to relax while eating tasty food, for fine food encourages pleasant table talk and a congenial atmosphere. There is scientific agreement on the point that food should be tasty and enjoyable in spite of diet restrictions.

Seasonings can do much to redeem the foods for those people on salt-free diets. Black Pepper has long been recommended for seasoning salt-free foods. In addition to aiding digestion, this spice actually helps promote good appetite; natives of India drink an infusion of Pepper for that very reason. Garlic Powder is another seasoning the dieter often finds especially satisfying.

The Council on Foods and Nutrition of The American Medical Association published a report in *The Journal* (the Association's official publication) of March 22, 1952, concerning the salt content of spices "because of the wide current interest in low-sodium diets and the uses of spices in such diets." Pointing out that low-sodium diets are now accepted treatment for a number of ailments, including high blood pressure, the report gave details of tests that had been conducted by the Department of Biochemistry of the University of Wisconsin which revealed that "with the exception of Celery Flakes and Parsley Flakes the amount of salt contributed through the usual amounts of spices used is insignificant, and that most spices can be used safely in low-sodium diets."

The dieter is faced with an ordeal, but one that spices can help him endure. Light, aromatic seasonings may also be the solution to the child who is an uninterested eater. He reaches eagerly enough for a fragrant Nutmeg cookie!

HOW TO USE SEASONINGS . . .

The uninitiated cook can learn to use the numerous seasonings which are available today in the same easy way she learned to use Vanilla, Salt, and Pepper—through her tasting spoon. Although it is established that certain foods and seasonings are compatible with each other (as Nutmeg in custard pie), a light touch and an adventuresome attitude toward cookery are the only prerequisites for concocting delicious foods.

"A light touch" means using seasonings so lightly that they cannot be instantly identified on first taste of the food in which they are used. When seasonings are used very skillfully only the gourmet will be able to distinguish the various flavors blended into a food.

"An adventuresome attitude toward cookery" means trying unusual uses and blends of the same old seasonings.

A few more specific how-to-use seasoning suggestions will help get the inexperienced cook off to an appetizing start:

1. When using *dried* herbs, start with ¼ teaspoon of an herb (or a blend of several) to a pound of uncooked meat, or to five or six servings of other food. A teaspoon of minced *fresh* herbs may be used to the same proportions of food. (Almost all dried herbs—Chervil and Tarragon are two of the few exceptions—are *much* stronger in flavor than green herbs.) After experimenting, you may prefer to increase or decrease these suggested quantities.

2. Use only *one* strong-flavored seasoning (Rosemary, Sage, Winter Savory, etc.) in a food. However, a strong-flavored seasoning may be combined with several mild-flavored ones (Chervil, Chives, Parsley, Summer Savory, etc.) for delightful dishes. Although not pungently flavored, Basil, Mint, Dill, Marjoram, Tarragon, and Thyme are among the herbs that are strong-flavored enough to give a good flavor flair to food; these accent herbs may be used either alone or in blends with more mild-flavored seasonings.

3. Although there is considerable difference of opinion concerning what is the best time to add seasonings to food, many experienced cooks recommend adding them as follows:

Long-cooking foods. Add seasonings to stews, soups, etc., during the last 45 to 60 minutes of the cooking time.

Quickly-cooked foods. Mix fresh herbs right in with the other ingredients, but soak dried herbs in a bit of milk or salad oil a half-hour before blending them into food that can be cooked in a few minutes' time.

Cold beverages. Add seasonings to vegetable juices, etc., 24 hours before serving and let stand in the refrigerator.

Salad dressings. Let dried herbs stand in unchilled oil dressings a couple of hours and then chill lightly before serving. For use in mayonnaise and other creamy dressings, blend the herbs into the dressing several hours before serving time. When a salad dressing *has* to be prepared on a moment's notice, add a little oil to the herbs and mash them thoroughly with the back of a spoon before mixing them into the dressing.

Although these suggestions can get the new cook off to a savory, safe start, she will soon have her own ideas about using seasonings and will be adapting these "rules" to suit her own taste.

HOT WATER BATH FOR DRIED HERBS . . .

If you like lightly-seasoned food you'll like a hot water bath for dried herbs. The heat and the moisture help loosen their flavorful oils and also lighten their flavor. Place the measured herb in a small tea strainer and dip it into scalding water for a few seconds; then quickly in and out of cold water. Drain the herbs well before mixing them into creamed food or salad dressings.

HERB BUTTERS . . .

A tasty take-off for the novice herb cook is herb butter. Use two tablespoons of minced green herbs (or about two teaspoons of dried ones) to a stick of butter. Cream the butter until light and then blend in the herb and a few drops of lemon juice. Let the butter stand in the refrigerator one day before using. This spread is delightful for embellishing sandwiches or for seasoning broiled meats. It keeps well, too, but for long-keeping freeze it in well-sealed jars. Although either salted or sweet butter may be used for making herb butters, sweet butter is more flavorful for this purpose.

PRESERVING HERBS . . .

If your garden boasts some herbs, freeze a supply of green ones to give your food a garden-fresh flavor when the snow flies. The fresh sprigs should first be dipped quickly in and out of boiling water and then cold water and be sealed and frozen immediately. For use in the not-distant future, simply mince the fresh herbs and fold them in little aluminum foil envelopes (one "serving" to each envelope) and freeze.

A few generations back green herbs were often preserved by salting. This method is favored even today by an occasional fine cook. Layers of a green herb and heavy salt are placed alternately in little jars. The salt-topped jars are then sealed and stored in a cool, dark place.

For centuries herbs have been cured by drying. Usually they are scattered loosely on screens, but home growers often hang herbs in loose bunches to dry in the attic, or some other dark, dry place. The French prefer to cure herbs in a slightly warm oven.

HOW TO SAVE ON YOUR SPICE BILL . . .

If the aromatic oils of herbs and spices evaporate, their flavors have gone the way of the oils, for the oils ARE the flavors. Sniff each can or jar of your seasonings occasionally to see if the delicate, distinctive aromas are still there. (No two spices have exactly the same fragrance or flavor.) If their aromas have faded your spices need replacing. However, with only a little care, spices will keep indefinitely:

1. Keep the jars tightly covered. (If you use the can type, close the sifter holes after each use.)

2. Keep all seasonings in a clean, dry place as far from the stove or other heat as possible.

3. Keep your spices dry, for moisture promotes caking and deterioration. (*Never* dip a moist spoon into a spice jar.) Discard spices that have begun to cake; it is folly to feel you must finish using a can of spice once it has begun to deteriorate.

FROM COOK TO CHEF . . .

The cook who loves to cook, naturally, does the most to advance the preparation of good food, for only she has the urge to experiment and come up with new taste sensations. And what fun she has observing her family's increased appreciation of her dishes that have been made more flavorful and fragrant through her imaginative use of seasonings! (It's a wise cook who doesn't give out advance publicity concerning her culinary experiments.)

To the dedicated cook seasonings are still as valuable as gold and precious jewels. She treats both with the same restrained respect, knowing that only a bit of her kitchen jewels is needed to add taste sparkle to her daily dishes.

Given an opportunity, these taste-tempters will soon convince even the most uninterested cook that cooking can be FUN. And, truly, as someone long ago observed, it is through the skillful use of seasonings that a cook gets promoted to the chef class.

Here are ideas, both old and new, to entice you into concocting more savory food. With this guide to encourage you as you add and taste, may your culinary creations be a tasty tribute to your Grandmother's sound rule: *Season to Taste!*

Seasonings

❧❦❧

ALLSPICE
(Spice)

❧❦❧

"Abracadabra!" said over the Baked Bean Pot won't help nearly so much as an atom of Allspice in the *beans.*

Allspice tastes like a blend of several spices. It *is* a blend of several flavors, mixed by the delicate hand of an expert, Mother Nature. This spice tastes like a combination of Cinnamon, Nutmeg, and Cloves—hence its confusing name.

Allspice is the ground dried fruit of the evergreen pimento tree (not the pepper *pimiento*) and has the distinction of being the only major spice grown exclusively in the Western Hemisphere. Jamaica, Guatemala, Mexico, Brazil, and the Leeward Island export this heavy-tasting, heavy-colored spice.

Allspice is invaluable for spicing up the *Mincemeat* (along with Cinnamon and Cloves), *Stewed* or *Baked Fruit* (especially *Apples*), *Spaghetti Sauce, Red Cabbage, Carrots, Eggplant, Ravioli, Split Pea Soup, Tomato Soup* and *Sauces, Barbecue Sauces, Relishes, Preserves, Pickles, Holiday Plum Puddings, Cookies, Spice* and *Fruit Cakes*—and *Fruit Salad Dressings!*

This flavor can also give special savor to *Boiled Fish (Cod, Halibut, Haddock, Red Snapper,* etc.), *Egg Dishes, Goulashes, Pot Roasts, Beef Soups* and *Stews, Ragouts,* and *Brown Gravies.* Whole Allspice is most often used in *Pot Roasts, Spiced Fruits, Preserves,* and *Pickles.*

A whisper of Allspice over the *Broiling Steak* will make a chef of the light-fingered cook who remembers.

My Favorite ALLSPICE Recipe

CRISP SWEET PICKLES FROM CANNED SOUR PICKLES

Drain the liquid from a quart jar of large whole sour pickles. Slice the pickles crosswise and return them to the jar alternately with a mixture of 2 cups Sugar, 1 tablespoon Whole Allspice, and 1 teaspoon Whole Cloves. Pour 2 tablespoons Olive Oil over the pickles. Let stand in refrigerator at least a week before using. (As the pickles disappear, use the sirup to season cole slaw.)

ANCHOVY PASTE

For a satisfying midnight snack, blend a tiny blob of this murky paste into *Scrambled Eggs* (rather into the bubbling butter before adding the eggs).

This rich, salty, fish paste, which comes in a tube, is used, of course, to make nippy *Canapes* and to season *Cream Cheese Spreads* and *Salad Dressings*. One inch of it in the *Butter Sauce* for *Broiled Steak* or *Fish* is reminiscent of the mysteries of the depths of the ocean.

If you aren't already an Anchovy Paste addict, a bright beginning can be made by using a bit of the paste on the *Boiled Egg Sandwich* for the lunch box. A teaspoon of the paste in *French Dressing,* along with grated hard-boiled egg yolks, makes an excellent dressing for *Shrimp Salad*.

Anchovy Butter (blend enough of the paste into creamed butter to suit your own taste) makes a zesty spread for *Hors d'oeuvres*. The English like Anchovy Sauce (Cream or White Sauce well-seasoned with this food accessory), but it's the French most of all who prize this salty savory.

Cost of the better brands rings high on the supermarket's cash register, but a little of the paste goes a long way, so use an artful hand in dispensing this potent paste.

And then there are Flat and also Rolled Anchovies for use as *Hors d'oeuvres*—or as a he-man garnish on *Green Salads*.

My Favorite ANCHOVY PASTE Recipe

CRAB FILLING FOR TOMATOES

½ pound Crab Meat   1 tablespoon Lemon Juice
¾ pound Cream Cheese   1 tablespoon Minced Parsley
½ cup Heavy Cream   ¼ teaspoon Worcestershire
⅛ teaspoon Flavor Salt   Sauce
½ cup Mayonnaise   1 teaspoon Anchovy Paste
  1 tablespoon Minced Onion   ⅛ teaspoon Tabasco Sauce
             1 Clove of Garlic, minced

Cream the Cheese until fluffy, and blend the Cream into it slowly. Then stir in the Mayonnaise gradually. Add the seasonings. Then fold in the Crab Meat. Use a small ice cream scoop to place a mound of the filling inside Tomatoes that have been cut not-quite-through in six sections.

ANGELICA
(Herb)

❧❧❧

"The Herb of the angels," Angelica is called, for it is said to protect those who use it from harm. A more earthly description is this: "The candied, colored (often green) leafstalk, roots, and stems of a biennial herb of the carrot family."

Angelica's flavor is somewhat like that of licorice. Candied Angelica—the herb's most popular form—is used to decorate *Desserts* and *Confections;* it is also served as a *Tidbit.* Most Candied Angelica is imported from France; this form is available from confectioners, herb dealers, and some drug stores.

The plant's leaves, blossoms, and stems are steeped in boiling water to make a flavorful *Tea.* The fresh herb is also used to season *Boiled Fish* (*Whitefish, Halibut, Cod,* etc.), *Preserves, Cakes, Candies, Fruit Salads,* and *Boiled Ham.* The green plant, which will grow in the home garden, is also eaten fresh.

Many cooks who know the value of a final thoughtful touch to foods depend on Angelica to give it.

ANISE
(Herb and Seed)

The black licorice sticks of childhood are brought to mind by this flavor, one that is especially popular with German cooks.

The fruit of this Parsley-family annual dry to form seed which are used to make mouth-watering *Candies; Cottage* and *Cream Cheese; Stews, Sausage, Shrimp, Hard-Shelled Crab; Beverages* (especially *Hot Milk* or *Tea Drinks*); *Cookies (Springerle!), Coffee Cake, Apple Pie; Breads; Sweet Pickles; Applesauce.*

The best Anise Seed come from Spain, Mexico, India, China, North Africa, and Asia, although Anise can be grown from fresh seed in almost any garden. Flavoring extract is made from the oil of the seed. Try a dainty drop of Anise Extract on *Cube Sugar* for the after-dinner *Coffee.*

Anise's green leaves are used sparingly to season *Fish* and *Cream Sauces; Tossed, Vegetable, Waldorf,* and *Fruit Salads; Cakes; Vegetable Soup,* and *Seafoods* (the leaves go into the cooking water). The green leaves are also used as a *Garnish.*

Anise *Tea,* made from either fresh or dried leaves, is said to induce sleep. Anisette, an Anise-flavored liqueur, is a favorite of the Spanish.

This ancient herb is mentioned by Jesus in Matthew 23:23: ". . . ye pay tithe of Mint and Anise and Cummin . . ."

Theophrastus, the Greek philosopher and naturalist, mentioned this herb in his writings. Charlemagne had it grown in his imperial gardens in the ninth Century. Pliny, Roman naturalist and author, also cherished it. The Romans used to hang an Anise plant near their pillows to ward off bad dreams—and to restore their youthful good looks. They also believed holding a sprig of Anise warded off epileptic seizures.

Anise's choice flavor was popular in *Spice* or *"Seed" Cakes* served at Roman holiday feasts. Today, ¼ teaspoon of Ground or Crushed Anise Seed in the dough for any *Rolled Cookie* will make Mother a more popular cook.

My Favorite ANISE SEED Recipe

ANISE REFRIGERATOR COOKIES

1 cup Butter or Margarine	1 cup Pecans, chopped fine
2 cups Brown Sugar	3½ cups Flour (all-purpose)
2 Eggs, well beaten	2½ teaspoons double-action
1 tablespoon Crushed Anise	Baking Powder
Seed	¼ teaspoon Salt

Cream the Shortening very light and add the Sugar gradually. Beat the Eggs in thoroughly. Add Nuts and Anise Seed. Sift dry ingredients together and add gradually to the creamed mixture. Shape into a roll 1¾″ in diameter. Wrap in waxed paper, and chill thoroughly. Cut in ⅛″ slices, and bake on a lightly-greased cookie sheet 10 to 12 minutes at 350° F.

SPICE ISLE

Sift the dry ingredients together 3 times, and add them alternately
to the flavor-mixture with the Buttermilk. Stir in Boiling Water,
bake in a hot (F) 375° oven 30 minutes, or until firm. Frost with Chocolate Icing, dusted over with ...

APPLE PIE SPICE
(Blend)

This fragrant blend can take the guess out of getting any *Apple
Dish* just right—*Pie, Dumplings, Applesauce, Brown Betty,
Strudel, Baked Apples, Candied Apple Rings,* and *Apple Snow.*

An unusually fragrant Cake can be made by adding two teaspoons of this spice to your favorite *Upsidedown Cake* recipe
and using Candied Apple Rings for the fruit. (Red or Green
Maraschinos go in the centers of the rings.) This blend is also
a tasty addition to *Whipped Cream* for topping any dessert.

Apple dishes rank high on the list of good foods men like.
Flavored with Apple Pie Spice, they can easily move to first
place.

My Favorite APPLE PIE SPICE Recipe

SPICY DEVIL'S FOOD CAKE

1 cup Butter or Margarine	1 teaspoon Soda dissolved in
3 small Eggs	1 cup Buttermilk
2 cups Sugar	4 ounces Chocolate, melted
3 cups sifted, all-purpose Flour	1 tablespoon Apple Pie Spice
½ cup Boiling Water	⅛ teaspoon Salt

Cream Shortening, and add the melted, cooled Chocolate. Beat Eggs
until light, and add Sugar to them; then add to creamed mixture.

Sift the dry ingredients together 3 times, and add them alternately to the Butter mixture with the Buttermilk. Stir in Boiling Water. Bake in three 9″ layer pans 30 minutes at 350° F. Frost with Chocolate Icing.

❦❧

BALM or LEMON BALM
(Herb)

❦❧

"Makes the heart merry and joyful," says an old Arabian proverb of Balm Tea. The Orientals claimed only that it soothed their nerves, but then they are always a conservative people. Literature makes numerous references to Balm's healing qualities, but, at the moment, we're interested chiefly in Balmy cooking.

The sharp-lemon-scented leaves of this perennial, which is native to Southern Europe, are used—fresh or dried—to give a tasty touch to *Green* or *Fruit Salads, Soups, Steaks, Roast Lamb, Fish, Sauces, Poultry Dressings, Hot* or *Iced Tea, Lemonade,* and *Fruit Punches.*

Good as *Tarragon Vinegar* is, it can still be improved—by a tiny touch of Balm.

The best way to have fresh Balm leaves for *Salads, Fruit Cups,* and *Wine Cups* is to start a bed of Balm from a root division.

My Favorite BALM Recipe

DRESSING FOR TURKEY

4 cups Soft Bread Crumbs
2 cups crumbled Corn Bread
1 teaspoon Salt
¼ teaspoon Pepper
½ teaspoon Balm
1½ teaspoons Sage
3 tablespoons Chopped Onion
3 tablespoons Minced Parsley
½ cup finely chopped Celery
2 grated hard-boiled Eggs
¾ cup Melted Butter or Margarine
1 cup Turkey Stock (or a Chicken Bouillon Cube dissolved in boiling water)

Combine the ingredients. Use to stuff a small Turkey, or bake in a well-greased pan.

❦❦❦

BASIL or SWEET BASIL
(Herb)

❦❦❦

Italian cooks dote on this easy-to-grow herb and use it with gay abandon in *Tomato Sauces*. (In Italy, this plant is a symbol of love; a sprig of it bespeaks the giver's fidelity.) One-fourth tea-spoon Basil in your usual *Sage Dressing* will have you, too, doting on this seasoning.

If you have a window pot of Basil (strong-flavored Italian and Curly Basils are especially adaptable to window pots), you've already discovered what a delight the fresh leaves are in a *Tossed Salad*.

Like Italian and Curly Basils, Dwarf and Lemon are also Sweet Basils—all at home in the kitchen. Basil's warm, sweet flavor reminds one of both licorice and cloves.

Basil is truly the "Tomato Herb," for its stimulating flavor and aroma are excellent in any dish calling for raw or cooked *Tomatoes*. The shiny green leaves of this annual of the Mint family are used, fresh or dried, whole or ground, to give character to:

Soups (especially *Tomato, Minestrone, Bean, Potato, Turtle, Oxtail*, and *Spinach*);

Vinegar for *French Dressing*; *Aspics*; *Creamed Butter* for *Sandwiches*;

Cottage or *Cream Cheese, Cheese Sauces, Welsh Rarebit, Cheese Soufflés*;

Scrambled Eggs and *Egg Dishes*;

Lima Beans, Green Beans or *Peas, Turnips, Green Peppers, Carrots, Eggplant, Zucchini, Onions, Squash, Tomatoes, Potatoes, Cauliflower, Cucumbers*;

37

Rice, Noodles, Spaghetti, Macaroni, Pizza Pie;

*Beef Stew, Lamb, Ham, Duck, Goose, Grouse, Venison, Pheas-
ants, Liver, Chicken, Steaks, Hamburger, Rabbit, Pork, Veal,
Stuffings, Milk Gravies;*

Shrimp, Mackerel, Halibut, Seafood Salads;

Green or *Vegetable Salads, Chicken Salad.*

Choice *Lamb Chops* will be even more elegant when sprinkled
lightly with Basil before broiling.

Basil Honey is an epicurean delight.

In India, to which country Basil is native (it is now grown on
the North Mediterranean Shore), the Hindus grow pots of Basil
in memory of their beloved dead and also to insure the grower's
own happiness. Ancient Greeks cherished Basil as the "Herb of
Kings." (Basil in Greek means king.) *Herbe royale* is the
French's respectful name for it. In Old England during Queen
Mary's reign, a visiting VIP was presented with a pot of Basil.
Back to the French and cooking, they use Basil especially in
Soups, Meat Pies, and *Stews.*

You can make your own Basil Vinegar by adding 3 tablespoons Dried Basil to a quart of boiling Red Wine Vinegar.
Cover tightly and let stand two or three days. Then strain, bottle,
and seal. Basil-accented Vinegar can be the secret of your delectable *French Dressing*—or of your wonderful *Whipped Potatoes.*

My Favorite BASIL Recipe

SCALLOPED EGGPLANT

3 cups cooked Eggplant pulp	¼ teaspoon Basil
1 medium Onion, minced	1 tablespoon Lemon Juice
1 Egg, well beaten	3 tablespoons Olive Oil
1 cup dry Bread Crumbs	½ cup grated Parmesan Cheese
½ teaspoon Flavor Salt	¼ cup thin Cream

Combine ingredients, and pour into a greased casserole. Top with additional Crumbs, and drizzle 1 tablespoon Olive Oil over Crumbs. Bake 30 minutes at 350° F. or until nicely browned.

BAY LEAF or LAUREL LEAF
(Herb)

❧❦❧

Walk all around a Bay Leaf and consider it carefully before using it whole. Moisture and heat will make its flavor rise like an unfriendly giant genie from the bubbling pot. Too-heavy use (often synonomous with a whole leaf) of this seasoning in *Beef Stew* will make you allergic to Beef Stew—and Bay Leaf—for the rest of your meals. Yet, used lightly, Bay Leaf can make an ordinary Stew extraordinary. Every cook should strive to establish rapport with this member of her kitchen corps.

Sauerbraten, Hasenpfeffer, and *Spiced Shrimp* are some of the few foods that can stand up under the flavor weight of three or four of these shiny beauties. Look with suspicion upon other recipes calling for plural portions of Bay Leaf.

But don't be bayed by this seasoning. Cut down to size, it's just as wonderful as the Romans thought (they baked *Wedding Cakes* on beds of the fresh leaves). Carefully controlled, Bay Leaf can make culinary marvels of:

Meat or *Tomato Aspics;*
Vegetable or *Fish Soup, Tomato Sauces, Gravies;*
Kidney, Game, Braised Oxtails, Heart, Tongue, Beef, Veal, Sausage, Chicken, Boiled Seafoods, Mutton, Pot Roast, Ham, Corned Beef;
Pickles, Tomato or *Mixed Vegetable Juices;*
Rice Dishes, Green Beans, Eggplant, Artichokes, Carrots, Beets, Kidney Beans, Boiled Potatoes, Tomato Dishes (especially), *Onions, Asparagus.* (Just see what Bay Leaf can do for the canned!)

All Pickling Spice contain a safe proportion of Whole Bay Leaf. The ground form of this leaf is easier to control in all-around cookery, but for some reason it is more difficult to find.

These dried leaves of the evergreen sweet-bay (laurel) tree are imported mostly from Turkey, Yugoslavia, Portugal, and Greece, although some come from California. The trees are often seen growing in yard tubs in the South. (Although the leaf of a large tree, this seasoning is popularly classed as an "herb.") The Greeks called the tree *Daphne* after the daughter of their River King Peneous, for she was changed into a laurel tree when being pursued by Apollo.

Some leaf, perhaps even Bay, probably accounted for the discovery of the art of seasoning food. A prehistoric man of perhaps thirty thousand years ago, historians think, may have wrapped his meat in leaves to protect it from the ashes in the fire pit in which he was cooking the meat. Later, when eating the meat, the man was pleasantly surprised to find the leaves had imparted a deliciously different flavor to his food, so the search for seasonings was on.

Latin primers are often enlivened by pictures of Roman politicos wearing crowns of waxy Bay Leaves. Our cooking days are made livelier by a little friendly fencing between Bay Leaf and our tasting spoon. But this leaf can easily be conquered to serve also as the cook's symbol of victory.

My Favorite BAY (LAUREL) LEAF Recipe

LOBSTER CASSEROLE A LA COSTA

2 cups cooked, chopped Lobster Meat
¼ cup Butter or Margarine
2 medium Onions, chopped
1 Clove of Garlic, minced
1 small Bay (Laurel) Leaf
¾ teaspoon Flavor Salt
½ teaspoon Cumin Seed, crushed or ground
¼ teaspoon Black Pepper
1 8-ounce can Tomato Sauce
1 cup Water
3 cups cooked Rice

Simmer Onions and Garlic in Melted Shortening until tender. Add Cumin Seed, Salt, Pepper, Bay Leaf, Tomato Sauce, Water, and bring to a boil. Add Lobster Meat, and let come to a boil again. Add Rice. Pour into buttered casserole. Dot with small pieces of Butter or Margarine. Bake 10 minutes at 350° F.

(This recipe, which is an unusually tasty use of Bay Leaf, was developed by my friend, Mrs. Gelsemira Costa, a seafood authority, of Groton, Connecticut.)

❧❧❧

BEEF EXTRACT

❧❧❧

A tiny (2¼-ounce) jar of this amber essence seems high-priced to the new user, but that little jar will enrich, flavor, and color many a pot of *Stew, Soup,* or *Chili.*

With this concentrate of meat essence, spices, salt, sugar, caramel, etc., on hand, you've always got the "makings" of good *Gravy.*

Let this good-as-gold seasoning also add chef-quality to *Spaghetti Sauces, Meat Loaf, Meat Balls, Grits,* and even *Corn Bread.* We know a hostess who adds a bit to *Cream Cheese* for canapés.

But watch the Salt when you're using Meat Extract. Since it is quite salty, you may need to reduce the Salt called for in any recipe you are improving with this seasoning. Also, too much of the essence gives food a scorched flavor. The quantity recommended on each jar is *enough.*

My Favorite BEEF EXTRACT Recipe

MEAT LOAF IN BLANKET

2 small Onions, chopped	½ cup Milk
Bacon Drippings	1 tablespoon Beef Extract
2 cups finely chopped Boiled Potatoes	⅛ teaspoon Black Pepper
1 tablespoon minced Parsley	Baking Powder Biscuit
1½ cups chopped cooked Meat	Dough made with 2
2 Eggs, beaten	cups Flour

Brown Onion in Bacon Drippings. Add Potatoes, and mix well. Add other ingredients, and heat thoroughly.

Roll Biscuit Dough into a rectangle about ¼ inch thick. Place the hot Meat Mixture in loaf form on the dough, and draw dough up over to form a roll. Moisten edges of dough, and press firmly together. Place on a lightly-greased cookie sheet, slash top of loaf, and bake 20 minutes at 425° F. Serve with Mushroom Sauce made by thinning a can of Condensed Cream of Mushroom Soup with ⅓ cup milk, and heating thoroughly. Garnish with Paprika and Parsley.

BERGAMOT or WILD BERGAMOT
(Herb)

Fresh sprigs of this lemon-fragranced plant are used to garnish *Wine Cups* and *Fruit Punch Bowls*. And that's the gayest thing we can say about it.

The French use Bergamot as a flavoring but especially prize the extracted oil in their perfumes.

There are several species of this Mint-family herb, which can be grown from either seeds or root divisions. Like any Mint, Bergamot's growth must be curbed by enclosing the bed with boards or brick to keep the plants from taking over. This herb can be found growing wild as far south as North Carolina.

When the Colonists boycotted English imports, the tea shortage caused a headache which Bergamot tea (adopted from the Oswego tribe) helped cure. Even today one of this herb's most popular uses is that of making a delightfully fragrant *Tea*.

BITTERS

This strong herb-flavored compound is best known at cocktail bars, but it is coming into popular use for giving a tantalizing touch to *Cream Soups* (especially *Mushroom*), *White* or *Cream Sauces, Gravies,* and *Cream Cheese Spreads* for hors-d'oeuvres.

When measured by the drop this concentrate will be worthy of your trust. Three drops to a three-ounce package of Cream Cheese is right for this cook's taste.

My Favorite BITTERS Recipe

STUFFED CELERY

Cream a 3 ounce package of Cream Cheese, and stir into it 1 teaspoon Cream. Then add 2 tablespoons very finely chopped cooked Mushrooms, 3 drops of Bitters, a bit of Cayenne, 1 teaspoon Lemon Juice, and Salt to taste. Fill small tender stalks from the heart of Celery with the Cheese Mixture. Garnish with Paprika or chopped Parsley.

(Professional looking Stuffed Celery depends on using a small pastry bag for filling the Celery.)

✥

BORAGE
(Herb)

✥

The oysterlike flavor of the young tender leaves of this annual can add personality to:

Potato Salad, Green Salads, Cream or *Cottage Cheese;*
Cucumbers, Cabbage, Green Peas and *Beans, Cooked Greens* (especially *Spinach*), *Lentils, Cauliflower, Tomatoes;*
Seafood Dishes, Meat Stews, Braised Beef;
Vegetable Soup, Cream Soups.

The dried leaves can be used in cookery just as the green ones are. Borage, a pretty plant with thick, grayish-green leaves, has a cucumberlike fragrance. Ancient Romans enjoyed the bruised leaves as a flavoring for their *Wine Cups;* today the leaves are preferred in *Drinking Water*—or *Tossed Salads.* Borage is frequently planted as bee pasturage that results in another fine honey.

Borage flowers often grace the *Punch Bowl;* they make a simple glass of *Lemonade* elegant. The lovely star-shaped blue flowers can be candied like violets to make a surprise appearance in cold January. Just brush the delicate beauties with egg white, then sprinkle well with finely granulated sugar, and let dry on a cake rack (in warm sunshine if possible). Store between sheets of waxed paper in air-tight containers. The flowers may also be dried plain for use in making *Tea.*

Sicily is blessed with an abundant growth of wild Borage.

You can have Borage in your garden if you begin with seed; this plant resents having its root torn up and moved. Once started, Borage handily re-seeds itself, assuring a continued supply of leaves for the *Salad* and the *Punch Bowls*.

BOUILLON CUBES

Dehydrated Beef, Vegetable, and Chicken Bouillon is available in cube form, usually packaged in small glass jars or tiny tube-like cans.

These flavorful cubes are used primarily to enrich *Soups, Stews, Gravies, Sauces,* and *Meat Pies,* but don't overlook these kitchen gems for enriching the cooking water for *Vegetables* —and *Grits!*

For a quick pickup, dissolve a cube in a cup of boiling water and sip it.

Bouillon Cubes have long been a favorite of cooks who know the cubes can make good food superlative.

My Favorite BOUILLON CUBE Recipe

CHICKEN AND VEGETABLE MOLD

1 envelope unflavored Gelatin
2 cups Water
2 Chicken Bouillon Cubes
1 cup cooked chopped
    Chicken

½ cup cooked Green Peas,
    drained
½ cup chopped Celery
2 Pimientos, chopped fine
1 tablespoon minced Parsley

⅛ teaspoon Thyme

Let the Gelatin soften in ½ cup cold water 5 minutes. Heat remaining water and dissolve Bouillon Cubes in it, stirring well. Remove water from heat, and stir in the softened Gelatin and Thyme. Chill until the consistency of unbeaten egg white. Fold in Chicken, Vegetables, and other Seasonings. Pour into a lightly oiled 4-cup mold, and chill until firm. Six servings. Serve with Mayonnaise.

❦❦❦

BOUQUET GARNI or KITCHEN BOUQUET
(Herb Combination)

❦❦❦

Sprigs of fresh herbs are often tied together in a "bouquet" or
placed in a small cheesecloth or muslin bag before being dropped
into cooking foods, such as *Stews* and *Soups*. It's easy to remove
the herbs then before serving the cooked food. Although bouquets are not always removed before the food is served, they
usually are. (*Fines herbes,* or minced herbs, always become an
integral part of the food in which they are used.)

A Kitchen Bouquet might contain tops and ends of Carrots,
Leeks or Green Onions, Sprigs of Parsley, Marjoram, Thyme,
Celery Tops, Tomato Peelings, Bay Leaf—and even a Whole
Clove or two. (There is a well-known sauce named "Kitchen
Bouquet," which is excellent for seasoning *Stews, Sauces,
Gravies, Pot Roasts,* etc.)

In France the term "bouquet" has a more specific meaning:
A *simple bouquet* may be as simple as a combination of Chives
and Parsley. A *bouquet garni* is a more elaborate combination
that might contain Celery Leaf, Parsley, Basil, Savory, Marjoram,
Onion, Bay Leaf, and Thyme. And a *soup bouquet* is the cook's
own pet concoction for making the soup kettle sing.

BROWNED FLOUR

This old cookery caper will stand revival, for Browned Flour is especially useful in making *Quick Gravies;* it both thickens and colors them. (Pasty, gray gravy puts the finger on the not-in-the-know cook.)

We don't buy Browned Flour; we make it.

Place Flour in a heavy skillet over very low heat, and stir constantly to keep it from scorching. When the Flour is evenly browned, cool it, and store in a covered jar.

For thickening a *Stew* or *Ragout,* blend some of the Browned Flour with a little Melted Fat, and stir the mixture into the hot food, and continue stirring until the food is evenly thickened.

This masterful gravy maker is praised by everyone who uses it; it guarantees no raw flour taste.

BURNET
(Herb)

❦❦❦

Burnet's light, cucumberlike flavor goes well in *Cream* and *Cottage Cheese, Spiced Vinegars, Summer Beverages, Cooked Greens, Vegetable* or *Green Salads, Mushroom* or *Asparagus Soup,* and—of course—in *Cucumbers.*

This flavor joins happily with those of Tarragon and Rosemary, so experiment a little with this trio.

Burnet was noted for its medicinal qualities some ages back. The crushed fresh leaves were used to treat soldiers' wounds; the Orientals used the dried leaves to help stop bleeding.

Burnet's tender shoots can "make" a *Green Salad*—superior. That one use justifies the effort of starting a small bed of this perennial which is native to Europe. Burnet will grow from either seed or root divisions. Then, a little later, the gardener will want to keep all the plants, except a few for seed, cut back to promote a lavish supply of the tender salad shoots. A few seasons later, Burnet will be growing "wild" in the neighborhood, for the seed easily escape from gardens.

On some slow afternoon, get out the tea pot and brew a little Burnet *Tea,* just as you would with any dried leaves. Let Lemon and Sugar join in the fragrant cup.

BUTTER

Down through the ages Butter has been considered the Queen of Seasonings. Without its delicate natural flavor no cook could produce the best in fine foods whether she be cooking *Vegetables, Meats, Sauces, Cakes, Pastries, Breads* or *Candies*.

Now many modern homemakers have discovered that quality vegetable Margarine provides flavor characteristics that allow Margarine to be interchanged with Butter in most recipes. The final decision as to which product to use will, of course, be up to you.

Pound Cake: There are lovely, light, fine-textured cakes made with vegetable shortenings and called "Pound Cakes," but *Traditional Pound Cake* is dependent on its full pound of Butter for its fine flavor. In making a white cake, the cook can choose between Butter which gives more flavor and shortening or other white fats which produce a whiter cake .

Browned Butter Icing is worthy of special mention; it is an uncooked icing that has the flavor of cooked icing. It's delicious on any kind of cake but seems especially harmonious with *Spice Cakes*:

Simmer ½ stick Butter over low heat until golden brown. Remove from heat, and blend into it 2 cups sifted Confectioner's Sugar, 3 tablespoons rich Cream, 1 teaspoon Salad Oil, and 1½ teaspoons Vanilla. Then blend in 1 tablespoon hot water, or enough to make the icing of spreading consistency. Spread the icing on cooled Cake. (If icing begins to get too stiff to spread easily, place it over hot water.)

And that superlative of pastries *Puff Paste* relies heavily upon Butter for its richness and flavor—a full cup of Butter to two cups Cake Flour and a half cup of water. (Your standard recipe book will give the directions for maneuvering these three ingredients into light pastry.) The French, who originated Puff Paste, use this rich dough as the basis of all their fancy pastries— Napoleons, patty shells, vol-au-vent cases, etc. The average home cook seldom takes the time to make Puff Paste, but those who do know that it is the most wonderful of all pastries.

Butter, is also a basic ingredient for *Cream* or *White Sauce* although Chicken Fat is sometimes used with excellent results. This is a good time to admit these two are acceptable substitutes for each other in much cookery, although Chicken Fat is inclined to be temperamental when used for baking, for the Fat is variable due to the diet of the chickens from which it came. (The best Pastry I ever tasted was made from a combination of Butter and Chicken Fat.)

Butter is an essential ingredient of *Hard Sauce* for topping the *Holiday Plum Puddings* and other *Steamed Puddings*: Cream 4 tablespoons Butter, and add slowly to it a cup of sifted Confectioner's Sugar, a tiny pinch of Salt, and a tablespoon of Sherry, Brandy, or Rum. Store in a covered jar in the refrigerator. When needed, spoon a halo of the solidified Sauce onto steaming-hot Pudding. (Also delicious on *Baked Apples*.)

Drawn Butter is simply melted Butter that has been poured off its settled Salt and Curd into tiny hot cups. Drawn Butter often accompanies *Boiled Shrimp, Lobster,* or *Crab*.

Almond Butter (crushed Almonds added to Drawn Butter) makes an elegantly simple dressing for *Hot Vegetables*—especially *Broccoli* or *Asparagus,* and also for *Broiled Fish*. (Sesame Seed are a happy substitute for the Almonds.)

Maître d'Hotel Butter (also called Drawn Butter by many cooks) may vary with the *"Maître d'Hotel,"* but the most popular version is melted Butter well-seasoned with Lemon Juice and Parsley or Chives. It makes a wonderful topping for *Hot Vegetables, Broiled Meats,* or *Boiled Sea Foods*.

Herb Butter is a stroke of sheer genius for raising *Sandwiches* from the humdrum to the glamorous: Cream a stick of Butter until light, and add 2 tablespoons finely-minced fresh Herbs (or 2 teaspoons of dried ones) and a dash of Lemon Juice. Don't overlook Herb Butter for seasoning *Hot Vegetables* and *Broiled Meats*.

Creamed Butter, plain or flavored, is the sandwich-maker's best friend. In addition to giving rich flavor, the butter also keeps the sandwich filling from soaking into the bread and making it soggy. *Sandwich* or *Canapé Butters* may be flavored with anything from A to Z: Anchovies, strong Cheese such as Roquefort, Chili Sauce, Chives, chopped Boiled Eggs, Garlic, ground Ham, Horseradish, minced Olives, Parsley, Poppy Seed, Pimiento, chopped Shrimp, Worcestershire Sauce, and other zesty zings.

CAMOMILE
(Herb)

❧❦❧

This perennial, which the Greeks called "Apple of the Earth," has an applelike fragrance.

Camomile has never been very popular in cookery. (The oil extracted from Camomile is used in tobacco and cosmetics.) So *Tea* talk is all we can offer at the moment.

A tisane, or tea, which is made from either fresh or dried leaves or flowers of this daisylike plant, is still served today in some European countries as a substitute for other hot teas or coffee. (It is said to reduce fever and to prevent infections in wounds, so Camomile Tea has long been a home remedy.) This tea is made as other herb teas are: Steep 3 teaspoons freshly-minced leaves (or 1 teaspoon of dried) in a cup of boiling water for three or four minutes. Serve with lemon and sugar.

Herb teas might well return. They bespeak an unrushed appreciation of life and a simple faith in Mother Nature's own healing methods.

CAPERS

CAPERS

Capers can't get by on their looks, but they can and do on their flavor. Tangy, salty, bitter Capers can add an exotic flavor and garnish to *Seafood Salads, Fish Sauces, Salad Dressings, Roasts, Canapés,* etc., but be miserly in using these dainty delicacies.

An ordinary *Head Lettuce* and *Mayonnaise Salad* becomes gala when garnished with these black-brown flower buds which have been pickled in Vinegar. The taste-exciting buds come from a plant that grows wild in the Mediterranean countries. Remember, young cook, the smaller the buds, the better their quality.

Pickled Nasturtium Seed look much like Capers and are an unpedigreed substitute for them. (See NASTURTIUMS.)

My Favorite CAPERS Recipe

EGG FOO YUNG

6 Eggs, beaten light	¼ teaspoon White Pepper
1½ cups chopped Ham	¼ teaspoon Worcestershire
⅔ cup finely chopped Onion	Sauce
¼ cup finely chopped Celery	1 tablespoon Soy Sauce
1 cup drained canned Bean Sprouts	1 tablespoon minced Parsley

Combine ingredients, and sauté in Butter, using a ¼-cup measuring cup for pouring mixture into skillet. Brown patties lightly on both sides, and serve promptly with Sauce:

1½ cups Chicken Stock (or dissolve 2 Chicken Bouillon Cubes in 1½ cups boiling water)

1 tablespoon Cornstarch

1 teaspoon Sugar

1 tablespoon Soy Sauce

2 teaspoons Capers and Juice

½ teaspoon Worcestershire Sauce

Combine ingredients, and boil for 3 minutes, or until slightly thickened.

Serve Egg Foo Yung with Buttered Rice, a Green Salad, and a light dessert.

CARAMEL

Caramel is both a flavoring and a coloring agent, one we make in our own kitchens.

Use Caramel generously to flavor *Cakes, Candies, Custard Desserts, Pie Fillings, Cake Frostings,* and *Ice Cream.* Use it lightly to color *Stews, Ragouts, Gravies, Soups,* and *Sauces,* and don't worry about Caramel sweetening these foods, for it isn't very sweet. (A bit of Sugar doesn't hurt *any* dish—seems to bind and blend the flavors.)

Caramel, or Burnt-Sugar Sirup, is made by slowly melting granulated Sugar in a heavy skillet over very low heat. The Sugar must be stirred constantly to keep it from scorching. ("Burnt-Sugar" is a misnomer, for care must be taken not to burn the Sugar.) You decide when to take it from the heat, for the darker the color, the stronger the flavor. (Many people like a good strong Caramel flavor.)

Proportions? For 1½ cups Caramel Sirup, melt 1 cup Sugar until browned to the degree you think you'll like. Remove the brown liquid from the heat, and slowly add 1 cup Boiling Water (Watch that steam!), stirring constantly. If you don't need all the Sirup immediately, cover and store the rest of it at room temperature.

A Custard dessert is sometimes baked in a Caramelized mold. One-half cup Sugar is browned directly in the mold, and the mold is then turned to spread the Caramel over it. Caramelized Sugar is sometimes used to garnish the same type desserts; it hardens quickly into delicious brittle threads.

In spite of rampant recipes to the contrary, the judicious cook knows that Brown Sugar does not give a genuine Caramel flavor —only *browned* Sugar does that.

My Favorite CARAMEL Recipe

CARAMEL DESSERT SAUCE

Bring to a boil 1 cup Granulated Sugar, 1 cup White Corn Sirup, 1 stick Butter. Add ¼ cup Sugar that has been caramelized and 1 cup Cream. Boil exactly 3 minutes longer, and remove from heat. Add 1 teaspoon Vanilla.

(Mrs. A. E. Lanier of Murfreesboro, Tennessee, passed this recipe on to me when I operated the dining room of the Stones River Country Club. There this rich sauce was popular served over Vanilla Ice Cream on Angel Food Cake, topped with Whipped Cream. The sauce will keep indefinitely in a covered jar in the refrigerator.)

CARAWAY
(Herb and Seed)

There's an affinity between the flavors of Apples and Caraway Seed. (Trinity College at Cambridge serves these crescent-shaped aromatics with *Baked Apples*.) Following through on that affinity, crush a teaspoon of the Seed with the back of a spoon, and add them to the *Waffle Batter*. Serve the crisp Waffles topped with *Hot Applesauce* that has been blended with much Brown Sugar and Melted Butter or Margarine.

We import these pungent seed in great quantity from The Netherlands, Indonesia, Denmark, Canada, and Lebanon, and use them to give excellence to:

Candies, Cookies, Pound Cakes;
Rye and *other Breads;*
Noodles;
Pickles, Pickled Beets;
Mutton, Roast Pork, Meat Stews, Liver, Kidney, Lamb (Sprinkle seed on meat before cooking);
Cheese Salads, Cheese Spreads for *Canapés;*
Asparagus, Creamed Onions, Boiled Red or *Green Cabbage, Sauerkraut, Cole Slaw, Turnips, Beets, French Fried Potatoes, Potato Salad;*
Clams, Oysters, Shrimp, Fish Chowders, Bisques (Use only a *few* Seed in these).

Although this perennial is native to Europe it is now grown widely in America.

Fresh Caraway Leaves are used sparingly in *Salads, Cauliflower, Cheeses, Cream Soups, Cabbage, Potatoes, Turnips, Roast Pork*. In Europe the yellow root of Caraway is relished as a *Vegetable;* it is said to have an especially good, sweet flavor, entirely different to that of the Seed.

Caraway *Tea* is sometimes called to the nursery to relieve colic (the seed have a slight laxative quality).

This, too, is an ancient herb. It grew in the imperial gardens of Charlemagne, who had seventy-four herbs on his list. Caraway Seed are another of the "meetin' seed" of our Colonial ancestors.

Dill Seed are sometimes substituted for Caraway Seed, even in sweet foods. But that's a negative note. Here's a positive one: Blend Cottage Cheese with Sweet Cream, Salt, Pepper, and a few spirited Caraway Seed. Serve in mounds on Lettuce. One of the best all-round salads I know. Women like it. Men like it. Children like Caraway Seed in their *Popcorn Balls*.

My Favorite CARAWAY SEED Recipe

SPICY SLAW

Soak a Cabbage Head in ice water for at least one hour. (A young Green Cabbage has more flavor and color appeal than a mature White one.) Drain well. Shave Cabbage finely with a long sharp knife. Add 1 small can drained Crushed Pineapple to the Slaw. Dice 1 unpared Red Apple and sprinkle with 1 tablespoon Lemon Juice, and add to Slaw. Brown 4 chopped slices of Bacon until crisp, and, while stirring, add 1 cup Wine Vinegar, ¼ cup hot water, 1 teaspoon Salt, ¼ teaspoon Pepper, 1 teaspoon crushed Caraway Seed, 1 teaspoon Sugar. Pour the hot Dressing over Slaw, and serve at once.

❦❦❦

CARDAMOM
(Seed)

❦❦❦

You may taste a Cardamom Seed in the *Demitasse* served by a thoughtful hostess. There's an affinity between the two (both ways), which is another reason *Danish Pastries* go so well with a cup of Coffee. (Their "different" flavor is Cardamom.) Some connoisseurs recommend a crushed Cardamom Seed in Scotch-on-the-rocks; I'll put my Cardamom Seed in *Apple Pie*.

Cardamom Seed can remedy that too-sweet sameness of *Strawberry Preserves*.

Whole pods of these delightful "grains of Paradise" can be purchased or just the tiny brown seed themselves, whole or ground. They are the dried fruit of a perennial native to India; we import the seed from Guatemala, Italy, and some from Central America, Mexico, and Ceylon. Spanish and Mexican cooks especially favor Cardamom Seed.

Cardamom's flavor (some people think it Aniselike) is intriguing in *Meats, Game,* and *Sausage.* One famous restaurant pounds Ground Cardamom into its *Steaks.* But it's especially worth the effort of digging the spice jar out when you're going to put Cardamom Seed in *Baked Apples, Coffee Cake, Melon Balls, Curries, Pickles, Honey, Mulled Wines,* and *Grape Jelly.*

This delightful spice, which may be used much as Cinnamon is, is found in all the better Pickling Spice, Curry Powders, and Sausage Seasonings.

On their way to church, our grandmothers often chewed these

sweet-smelling seed. Today one after a cocktail helps as much as anything else and is more pleasant than most such efforts. Even today the Arabs consider Cardamom Seed a good nibbling confection.

Blend a bit of Ground or Crushed Cardamom Seed into *Honey*, and use it to sweeten lightly buttered *Grapefruit Halves*. Broil. Serve as an elegantly simple dessert after a heavy dinner.

Coffee Gelatin, spiced with Cardamom Seed and topped with whipped cream, will please even the most bored palate.

Cardamom Seed is one of the more expensive spices—45c for ½ ounce in this year of 1955. But that's a year's supply if the cook doesn't get a seed and a pod confused. Six of the tiny dark seed from out of the miniature white pod are enough to flavor a dozen Danish Pastries, or *Pfeffernusse*, those German Christmas cookies.

My Favorite CARDAMOM SEED Recipe

GRAPE PIE

Stem 4 cups Concord Grapes, and slip the pulp out of the skins. (Reserve skins.) Cook pulp until seeds loosen, and then press pulp through a sieve to remove seeds. Combine pulp and skins with ¾ cup Sugar, ⅛ teaspoon Ground or Crushed Cardamom Seed, 1½ tablespoons Lemon Juice, 1 tablespoon each of grated Orange Rind and Quick-Cooking Tapioca. Mix well, and let stand 5 minutes. Pour into a 9″ pastry-lined pan. Cover with a lattice top. Bake 10 minutes at 450° F., and then lower heat to 350°, and bake 20 minutes longer. Serve with Whipped Cream.

✂❦✂

CATNIP
(Herb)

✂❦✂

Roasts were once rubbed well with the crushed fresh or dried leaves of fragrant Catnip. And tiny green sprigs of it often turned up in *Tossed Salads, Meat Stews,* and *Soups.*

Captain John Mason is thought to have started this herb, which will grow from either seed or root divisions, in America. Catnip quickly became popular for preparing a tonic, another *Herb Tea.* The Colonists passed the good word on to the Indians, who, after some experimenting, passed the word back that the tea induced sound sleep.

Catnip, a perennial, is no longer widely used in cookery. But what little girl has not force-fed her kitten Catnip Tea, a drink that is said to give courage and strength? (Many pet shops carry the dried leaves.) I can never pass a Catnip Plant without first stopping to enjoy nibbling a fragrant sprig of it.

CAYENNE
(Spice)

The cook who handles Cayenne too lightly is in the frying pan. Too heavily, she's in the fire. The judicious handling of red-hot, savory-flavored Cayenne is a positive identification of the born-to-cook cook.

This spice is the ground pod and seeds of various Chili Peppers grown in Africa, Mexico, Japan, Nigeria, and the United States. The peppers vary greatly in size. Although Cayenne is usually powdered, the whole peppers do appear in Pickling Spice.

Cayenne can enliven *Seafood* or *Chicken Salads, Green* or *Lima Beans, Turnips, Cooked Greens (Mustard, Turnip, Poke, Kale, Collards), Squash, Cauliflower, Soufflés, Tomato* and *Meat Aspics, Creamed Egg and Cheese Dishes, Cream Soups, Sauces,* and *all Meats,* but especially *Barbecued Beef, Pork,* and *Lamb.*

The secret of good *Shellfish Cookery* is Cayenne. (Cayenne is also the secret of how to end that pesty ant nest by the doorsteps.)

This extrovert seasoning resists measuring. It must be used "to taste." And, sensitive stomachs, beware!

For those of us who never tire of this mouth-burning spice, *Buttery Sauce* for any hot vegetable is too bland without it: Melt 3 tablespoons Butter or Margarine, blend in Cayenne to your taste, and add ¼ teaspoon Paprika.

Incidentally, heat brings out the hotness of Cayenne, so when using it, add ... stir ... and taste. And taste again five minutes later before adding more of the powerful pepper.

There are several types of Ground Red Pepper, each of which may be used much as Cayenne is. Whole Red Peppers are used primarily in pickles and relishes.

Next time you're having *Macaroni* and *Cheese,* add a good shake of Cayenne along with the usual Mustard. Let your tasting spoon say "when."

Used to give just the right bite to food, authoritative Cayenne is a tasty tribute to the cook. *Creamed Chicken,* for instance, is flat without this hot ingredient; yet we must not be conscious of Cayenne's presence in it—or in any other food. Except *Cheese Straws!*

A speck of fiery Cayenne, Mexico's most popular seasoning, can illuminate the flavor of an *Orange Soufflé.* (That's right, Cayenne improves *Sweet Soufflés.*) Used discreetly, Cayenne can neon-light the quality of all cookery.

My Favorite CAYENNE Recipe

CHEESE STRAWS

Cream 1 stick Butter or Margarine, and add to it 1 pound grated Sharp Cheddar Cheese that has been allowed to come to room temperature, 1 teaspoon Salt, ¼ to ½ teaspoon Cayenne, and 2 cups Flour. Put dough through a cookie press to form straws on an ungreased cookie sheet. (Or roll and cut with a pastry wheel.) 350-degree them to a delicate brown. With Salads or Cocktails, of course.

CELERY

Celery Seed are a prerequisite to *Potato Salad*. They are also delicious in *Soups, Beef Stew, Hamburgers, Onions, Cauliflower, Cole Slaw, Salmon Croquettes, Chutney, Pickles, Cheese Spreads, French Dressing,* and on *Toasted Crackers.*

The seed are available whole or ground and also as a Salt. Try Celery Salt in *Iced Sauerkraut Juice, Lima Beans, Chicken Salad, Soups, Scrambled Eggs, Oyster Stew, Cream Sauces, Roast Pork, Clam Juice, Tomato Juice, French Dressing,* or *Mayonnaise.* After tasting this flavored salt on your *Breakfast Eggs* you'll agree Celery Salt is worthy of its own silver shaker for table use.

Southern France, India, China, and the United States produce the small plant, similar to American Celery, from which Celery Seed come. The flavor of the seed is warm and slightly bitter, very much like that of fresh Celery.

Fresh American Celery is one of our most important seasonings. In addition to giving a fresh flavor to almost any *Meat* or *Vegetable Dish* and most *Soups,* chopped Celery also gives that important quality called "texture contrast." No matter how good-tasting, we soon tire of dishes that have no "body" to them. Chopped Fresh Celery can do for *Creamed Dishes* what grated Almonds do for Chicken Soup. Celery is at its best raw, for use in either *Salads* or *Creamed Dishes* (very finely minced for the latter use, or half-cooked). A little very finely chopped Fresh Celery improves a *Fruit Salad,* both its flavor and its texture.

Celery Flakes are made from dehydrated American Celery Leaves. Only the water has been removed; cooking restores much of the bulk and the color. You can make your own Celery Flakes from those too frequently discarded Celery tops. Dry the leaves in a warm oven for several hours, and then crumble them and store in tightly-covered jars. This seasoning is good-looking and good-tasting sprinkled over *Boiled Buttered Vegetables* (especially *Potatoes* or *Cauliflower*). Use the Flakes in any way you would Parsley, but especially in *Cream Sauces* and *Soups*. They can pinch-hit for *Salad* use when you find you're out of Fresh Celery.

Fresh Celery Leaves are tasty things chopped up in *Salads, Soups,* and *Stews.* (*Tossed Salads* neglect these leaves too often.)

The small root base of a Celery Stalk is a sweet, crisp delicacy, but since cook has first nibbling rights few other people ever get to taste it.

My Favorite CELERY FLAKE Recipe

CELERY FLAKE SAUCE

Mix well, and stir over low heat until the Sauce is thoroughly hot:

1 can condensed Cream of Chicken Soup	⅓ cup Milk
	1 tablespoon Celery Flakes

Cayenne to taste

This Sauce can grace many different foods—Macaroni Ring, Rice, Open-Faced Sandwiches, Fish, Croquettes, Fritters, and Meat or Vegetable Casseroles.

My Favorite CELERY SALT Recipe

"NUTS AND BOLTS"

Combine the following, and place in a large shallow baking pan:

4 boxes of Cereal of interesting but tiny shapes (not the sugar-coated type)	1 pound Pecan Halves
	1 pound Walnut Halves
	1 box Pretzel Sticks

2 cans Potato Sticks

Combine the following, and stir thoroughly into the Cereal Mixture, tossing well:

1½ cups Butter or Margarine   1 teaspoon Celery Salt
½ teaspoon Tabasco Sauce   ⅛ teaspoon Garlic Powder
              1 teaspoon Worcestershire Sauce

Bake at 200° F. for 3 hours or until crisp. Cool and store these cocktail tidbits in air-tight containers; the mixture will keep indefinitely. These snacks make interesting Holiday gifts.

My Favorite CELERY SEED Recipe

CREAM OF CELERY SEED DRESSING

⅓ cup Tomato Catsup   1 tablespoon Worcestershire
½ cup Mayonnaise   Sauce
2 tablespoons Prepared Mus-   1 teaspoon Celery Seed
   tard   Cayenne to taste

Combine the above ingredients, chill, and serve over Lettuce Wedges.

❧❦❧

CHERVIL
(Herb)

❧❦❧

Chervil's delicate Parsleylike flavor (some cooks say Tarragon-like) likes to go out with those of Basil and Chives.

The leaves of this annual of the Carrot family make an attractive *Garnish*, although they don't have the stamina of faithful Parsley.

Unlike many other herbs, Chervil's leaves don't get stronger in flavor when dried. (They're at their best fresh, of course.) This seasoning, which is available whole or ground, may be used as Parsley is in:

Cream Soups, Green Salads, Fried Eggs, Omelets;
Stews, Beef Dishes, Broiled Chicken, Carrots;
Peas, Spinach, Butter Sauces for *Fish, Cheese Dishes,* and *Stuffings.*

Roots of the tuberous type Chervil are cooked much as other root vegetables are—steamed or boiled.

Charlemagne grew Chervil. Pliny took time to record that this herb had been known to stop hiccoughs.

French cooks rely on Chervil in their *aux fines herbes*. You, too, can rely on Chervil, in all-around cookery.

My Favorite CHERVIL Recipe

VEGETABLE SAUCE

Combine the following ingredients, and heat over hot water:

⅓ cup Cream
½ cup Mayonnaise
1 Pimiento, chopped fine

1 teaspoon Dried Chervil (or 1 tablespoon freshly minced)

⅛ teaspoon Celery Salt

This simple sauce is especially tasty over Broccoli or Asparagus, but may be used over any hot vegetable at all.

CHICKEN FAT and CHICKEN STOCK

The rich yellow semi-solid fat that rises to the top of Chicken Stock can add golden goodness to *Vegetables, Sauces, Soups,* and *Baked Products,* including *Biscuits, Pastries,* and *Cakes.* (A Tennessee restaurant that is justifiably famous for its Apple Pie is said to use half-Butter and half-Chicken Fat in its Pastry.)

Seven-eighths cup Chicken Fat is equivalent to about one cup vegetable shortening. But there's a catch: Chicken Fat is variable, so success in baking with it often depends on experimentation—and experience. But there's no catch to using the Fat as a Butter substitute for seasoning vegetables, just any vegetable at all.

Chicken Stock has countless uses. Use it to make *Sauce* for any Creamed Dish, either meat or vegetable. *Soup Base* is its most popular use, but don't overlook this Stock as a water substitute in *Vegetable Cookery.* Soon you'll want Chicken Stock in everything!

Try this method for your next Baked Hen: Simmer the Hen gently in water to cover until almost tender. (Don't worry about that school of thought that says, "Cooking in water takes out the goodness." However, *boiling* will make the meat stringy, so keep the water at a gentle simmer.) When the Hen is almost tender, drain, brush with Fat, and finish cooking the fowl in the oven. Cooking a Hen entirely by dry heat can result in the loss of much golden Fat, making it too strong for use. By the simmer-then-brown method you'll have a tender, beautifully-browned fowl, *and* a pot of rich Stock. Never refrigerate Chicken Stock until it is thoroughly cool, or it will sour. Not quite full jars of Stock freeze well. The Fat freezes well. So treasure every spoonful of these rich seasonings, and use them to make incredibly delicious dishes.

CHILI POWDER
(Blend)

A touch of Chili Powder *in Cheese* or *Egg Dishes* makes them interestingly different; a touch *on* them is a little thing but one of those that count. *Chowders* urgently need Chili Powder's pep.

Chili Powder, which was used by the Aztecs back in the 14th Century, is still the most widely used seasoning in Mexico. This seasoning, which includes several kinds of Red Chili Peppers (whole, these Peppers are used to enliven *Tomato Relishes, Vinegars, Sauces, Stews*), and sometimes Oregano and Cumin Seed, dominates Mexico's national dish, *Chili con Carne (Chili with Meat)*. That dish is also popular in our Southwestern states and is sweeping into others. The success of many a small drive-in restaurant is founded on its good Chili—as also is the reputation of some prominent hostesses who enjoy the ease and informality of serving previously prepared Chili. (Former President Truman is reported to give Chili Parties.) Hostesses are also partial to Chili Powder in *Avocado Dips*.

Chili Powder is used for pointing up the flavor of many foods—

Beef Stew, Pot Roasts, Braised Beef, Stuffings, Shellfish Dishes (especially *Creole Shrimp*);

Spaghetti, Barbecue, Hot Dog, and *Seafood Cocktail Sauces;*

Corn Meal Mush, Hot Tamale Pie, Tamales;

Omelets, Scrambled Eggs;

Corn (Fresh or *Canned), Green Peas, Celery, Carrots, Egg-*

plant, Rice, Broiled Tomatoes, Green Peppers—any sweet vegetable;

Marinades and *Gravies*.

Chili Powder can vary from sweetly hot to *Hot,* so learn *your* spice packer. Incidentally, Black Pepper is usually omitted when a hot Chili Powder is used.

My Favorite CHILI POWDER Recipe

CHILI

2 pounds Ground Round Steak	4 tablespoons Chili Powder
1 Clove of Garlic, minced	2 teaspoons Salt
1 can Tomatoes	1 teaspoon Cumin Seed, crushed
1 can Red Kidney Beans	or ground

2 cups Hot Water with 2 Beef Bouillon Cubes dissolved in them

Brown the Ground Meat well in Bacon Drippings. Add the other ingredients, and simmer slowly 2½ hours. (For a thinner Chili, add Water or Tomato Juice.)

CHIVES
(Herb)

A sprinkling of chopped Chives can give a fillip to an otherwise insipid dish.

Chives—one of the most popular of all culinary seasonings—look like slender green onions but have a more refined flavor. The plants, with their lovely little lavender pompon flowers, are ornamental as well as tasty. In cookery, this delicate seasoning can go any place onions do, and oftener.

Just to start a Chives-flavored chain of thought—*Cream* and *Cottage Cheeses, Appetizers, Potatoes, Lima Beans, Fish, Green Salads, Egg* or *Cheese Dishes, Butter Sauce, Dressings, Soups, Vegetable Juices,* etc.

A Chives *Omelet* is a real supper treat.

A pot of Chives on the window-sill stands ready to give a finishing touch to many a menu and keeps you from being hampered by the brief December-to-March market for this miniature "onion." Many supermarkets carry pots of Chives. Chives need moderate water and sunshine; the plants should be cut often to make them grow. Their flavor is best before the blossoms appear. Dry surplus Chives, crush, and store in jars. The tiny bulbs are appealing pickled for use as *hors-d'oeuvres;* also, the little globes are grand in salads.

My *Favorite CHIVES Recipe*

CHEESE-STUFFED SALAD PEPPERS

Blend a generous quantity of minced Chives into Cream Cheese that has been whipped to a fluff with a bit of Mayonnaise. Fold in 1 finely-chopped Pimiento. Cut off just enough of the tops of Green Peppers to allow scooping out of seed and white membrane, and stuff the Peppers with the Cheese Mixture. Chill them well. Slice Stuffed Peppers into salad rings, and lay them on Tomato Slices on Lettuce for a hole-in-one salad.

$\sim$§§$\sim$

CHOP SUEY SAUCE
(Condiment)

$\sim$§§$\sim$

This exotic blend of "hydrolized vegetable protein, corn sirup, caramel, and spices" is intended primarily for dashing generously over *Chop Suey, Chow Mein,* and other *Chinese Dishes.* It adds a rare, piquant flavor to their blandness. What this sauce does for Chinese foods it can also do for American *Stews, Gravies,* and *Sauces.*

Here's an almost-new idea: Brush Chop Suey Sauce over the *Roasting Leg of Lamb*: gives it a gloriously brown, crusty coat that pleases both the eye and the palate.

CINNAMON

(Spice)

Try a sprinkling of Cinnamon in *Green Peas* or *Spinach*—or on top of the *Squash Casserole*. A pinch in *Chili* will bring exclamations of praise. But *Chocolate,* of course, is Cinnamon's most compatible companion flavor.

Some Eastern countries use Cinnamon in *Coffee,* not Cream and Sugar as we do. And we often use a stick of Cinnamon for stirring black after-dinner coffee. (Whole rolled Cinnamon bark is called "quills.") But, more frequently, we use Stick Cinnamon to give special significance to *Stewed Prunes, Peaches, Apples, Pears*—or *Hot Chocolate.*

Ceylon Cinnamon is the best flavored of Cinnamons, but Cassia, "Chinese Cinnamon," is usually substituted for true Cinnamon. In fact, many cooks prefer its stronger flavor. Cassia Buds, one of the first spices known, are found in Pickling Spice. True Cinnamon is usually found in stick form.

"Sweet Powder," as Cinnamon was known in ancient times, is widely favored in—

Apple Butter, Pickles, Catsup, Chili Sauce, Applesauce, Spiced Vinegar, Mulled Wines and *Cider, Spiced Tea;*

Raisin or *Apple Pie, Pears, Peaches, Compotes* of *Stewed Fruits, Mincemeat;*

Sweet Potatoes, Cream of Corn Soup;

Lamb, Pork Chops, Hams, Beef Stew, Meat Aspic;

81

Bread Pudding, Sweet Rolls, Waffles, Muffins, Chocolate Sirups and *Puddings.*

This spice, which was once a fit gift for monarchs, was thought in ancient times to inspire love, and a love potion was concocted from it. Today every child loves Cinnamon-flavored *Gelatin Candy,* a nourishing treat that many mothers favor over more rich-in-sugar candies:

Bring to a boil 1½ cups Sugar, a pinch of Salt, ¾ cup Boiling Water. Soften 2 envelopes of unflavored Gelatin in ½ cup Cold Water and add to the first mixture. Boil slowly 15 minutes. Remove from heat, and tint a delicate pink with Food Coloring. Add Cinnamon Extract to taste (about ½ teaspoon). Pour mixture into a 4″ x 8″ pan that has been rinsed with cold water. Let stand in a cool spot outside refrigerator for several hours. Then cut into bite-size cubes with a wet sharp knife. Toss the pink cubes in finely granulated sugar in a paper bag. Spread candy on a tray to dry for an hour or so, and then store in airtight containers.

The Old Testament mentions Cinnamon as an incense ingredient; this spice is still widely used in cathedrals today. The Romans burned it to curry favor with Mercury, their God of Commerce. Ancient Jews anointed the vessels of the tabernacle with Cinnamon-perfumed oils. Oriental women once perfumed their beds with this fragrance; Chinese records mention Cinnamon as far back as 2700 B.C.

The Arabs cornered the world market for Cinnamon for centuries by fabricating fearful stories of ferocious flesh-eating birds and monsters that attacked those seeking Cinnamon. Later when the Dutch were in control of the world spice market they burned Cinnamon when its price went too low to suit them.

There are a hundred different recipes for *Cinnamon Toast.* Here is one of the best:

Cream a stick of Butter or Margarine, and blend into it ½ teaspoon Vanilla, ½ cup sifted Confectioner's Sugar, 2 tablespoons Cinnamon, 1 teaspoon grated Orange Rind, and 2 tablespoons Applesauce. Spread the mixture on golden brown toast, and run the toast under the broiler long enough to melt the topping. Keep the unused Cinnamon Spread in the refrigerator ready for breakfast call. Also use it when you want a quick topping for Baked Apples.

A different dessert for the card club is something to think about. *Cinnamon Ice Cream?* Just blend 2 teaspoons Cinnamon into a pint of slightly-softened Vanilla Ice Cream, and refreeze in ice trays. Chocolate Sauce, of course.

A teaspoon of Cinnamon in the *Breakfast* or *Tea Muffins* adds spice to the chatter.

A *Cinnamon Roll* can be an enchanting geography lesson when served with Milk, a map, and, "Cinnamon comes from Ceylon to flavor your Sweet Roll."

My Favorite GROUND CINNAMON Recipe

1850 QUEEN CAKES

1 pound Butter or Margarine	1½ pounds Dried Currants, dusted with a little of the Flour
1 pound Sugar	
3½ cups sifted Cake Flour	
8 Eggs	1 teaspoon each Nutmeg and Mace
1½ tablespoons Brandy	
1 tablespoon Cinnamon	

Cream Shortening until very light, gradually adding the Sugar. Beat the Eggs in one at a time, beating well after each addition. Sift Flour with Spices, and add to the creamed mixture. Add Brandy, and then fold in the Currants. Fill individual 3″ pie pans ¾ full. Bake at 325° F. Make a thin frosting of Confectioner's Sugar, Cream, and Lemon Extract, and pour it over the cakes.

My Favorite STICK CINNAMON Recipe

RUSSIAN TEA

This is, by far, the best Russian Tea Recipe I have ever found. Mrs. Frank Eanes, a gifted cook, of Lakeland, Florida, passed it on to me.

> 5 sticks Cinnamon, broken in pieces
> 3 large pieces Ginger Root
> 3 tablespoons Whole Cloves

Put the above spices in 2 cups Cold Water and bring to a boil. Turn heat low, and let simmer 1 hour. Strain. Add 2 cups Sugar to the essence (and more water if the mixture has boiled very low), and boil for 3 minutes. Make 1 quart of moderately strong Tea (using about 3 Tea Bags), and add the Spiced Sirup to the Tea. Then add 2 quarts each Orange Juice and Pineapple Juice and the juice of one dozen Lemons (or 2 bottles of the Bottled Juice). Mix well, and let stand several hours. When ready to serve, heat the Tea slowly to the simmering point, but never let it boil.

CLOVES
(Spice)

Lemon Slices center-studded with Whole Cloves are seen on the prettiest tea tables, as are *Spiced Nuts* that are faintly redolent of Ground Cloves.

Ground Cloves are most frequently combined with other spices, but a sprinkling of this heavenly-scented powder goes well in—

Spice Cakes and *Cookies, Sugared Doughnuts, Gingerbread, Chocolate Desserts;*

Spiced Wine, Mulled Cider, Russian Tea, Fruit Punch, Cranberry Juice, Relish, or *Sauce;*

Broiled Pineapple Slices, Mincemeat, Preserves;

Potato, Tomato, or *Beef Soup, Borscht, Consommé;*

Green Beans, Onions, Harvard Beets, Candied Sweet Potatoes, Tomatoes (especially *Tomato Aspic*);

Baked Ham, Fresh Pork Roast, Fried Sausages, Stews, Meat Loaf, Stuffings, Hogshead Cheese, Corned or *Roast Beef, Baked Fish, Venison* and *other Game, Stewed Chicken.*

This old trick should be passed on to every young cook: Stud an Onion with two or three Whole Cloves, and drop it into the *Beef Stew* during the last hour of cooking. (Cloves-studded oranges and apples, the most ancient of spice balls, are still used to give fragrance to clothes and to discourage moths. See "Recipe.") One or two Whole Cloves in the steeping *Tea* are an interesting variation. Three in *Boiled Tongue* is the peak of piquancy. Incidentally, Whole Cloves are preferred in *Pot Roasts, Spiced Fruits, Preserves, Pickles, Teas,* and for studding the *Baked Ham.*

Chinese Court Officers of the Third Century used Whole Cloves as mouth-sweeteners. In fact, the officers were required to hold Cloves in their mouths while addressing their sovereign. Oil of Cloves has long been used to relieve toothache.

Cloves were first discovered in the Spice Islands (now called the Moluccas). There parents planted a Clove tree, which might grow to forty feet in height, in honor of each new child; death of the evergreen birthday tree was thought to foretell the child's own death. The Dutch cut down many such trees when in control of the Spice Islands, for they saved only the trees they could guard. Cloves, together with other spices, have cost dearly in human lives, for cruel wars were waged over the rich islands where fragrant Cloves were first found.

Lebanon, British West Africa, Mozansbique, and Madagascar supply us with these nail-like dried flower buds of the Clove tree.

Hotly sweet Cloves call for culinary carefulness, for both their color and their flavor are heavy. Be as miserly with this seasoning as you would if a pound of Cloves were still barter for two cows as in the Eleventh Century.

My Favorite GROUND CLOVES Recipe

PARTY PECANS

Dip Pecan Halves in an egg white that has been diluted with 2 tablespoons Cold Water. Then dip each nut in the following mixture after sifting the ingredients together:

¼ cup Cornstarch	½ teaspoon Ground Cloves
½ cup Sugar	⅛ teaspoon Salt

Bake the Nuts on a cookie sheet for 1¼ hours at 250°. Cool the nuts thoroughly (they will be crisp when cool), and store in airtight cans. This is another easy gourmet gift item.

My Favorite WHOLE CLOVES Recipe

POMANDERS (SPICE BALLS)

These can be a rainy afternoon activity that will keep the children amused and the closets and bureau drawers sweet-smelling for years.

Stick Whole Cloves into thin-skinned Oranges until they are entirely covered. Then roll the fruit in a 50-50 mixture of Ground Cinnamon and Orris Root, patting a heavy coating onto each Orange. Wrap the fruit individually in tissue paper, and let cure for six weeks. Remove tissue paper, and shake off the surplus powder. The Scent Balls are ready for use.

≈§❧≈

INSTANT COFFEE

≈§❧≈

If you like the flavor of Coffee, make the most of this fine powder as a food flavoring:

1. Blend a teaspoon of Instant Coffee into a pint of slightly softened *Vanilla Ice Cream*. Refreeze in ice tray. Serve with Chocolate Sauce.

2. For *Coffee Bavarian Cream,* add a teaspoon of Instant Coffee to any standard recipe for Bavarian Cream.

3. Add Instant Coffee to any *Chocolate Recipe* to make it Mocha—whether *Cake Frosting, Pie, Beverage,* or *Brownie.*

4. Fold two teaspoons of this powdered perfection into *Whipped Cream* for topping Chocolate Desserts—or Angel Pies.

5. Use the powder for making *Coffee Gelatin* (and don't forget a crushed Cardamom Seed).

6. Add a teaspoon of this concentrate to *Prepared Vanilla Pudding Mix* before blending in the Milk. (This Mix will be greatly improved if you add an Egg Yolk and also fold in the stiffly-beaten Egg White.)

7. Toss three tablespoons of this pulverized luxury into the ingredients for any *White Cake. Voila!* Genuine *Coffee Cake!*

You've got better ideas already. Carry on . . .

❧❧❧

COGNAC

❧❧❧

A teaspoon of Cognac in the *After-Dinner Coffee* will put you to wondering about other ways to enjoy this French Brandy, one that is made exclusively of Grape Wine.

Cognac is popular for flavoring *Puddings, Fruit Cups, Crab Dishes, Creamed Chicken, Omelets, Game* and other *Meats, Cheese Spreads,* and *Cheese Dishes.* Since Cognac is one of the ready-flaming liquors it is often used in preparing *flambée* dishes.

The secret of a lovely flaming dish eluded me for years. Mr. Herbert D. Young, a well-known Middle Tennessee dairyman and a hobby cook, revealed it to me: *Warm the Cognac before pouring it over a food.* Then touch a lighted match quickly. Presto—a flame *that* high! (But don't hope to ignite Cognac diluted in a sauced dish.)

Of all flaming dishes *Crêpes Suzette* is the best known. *Steak Diane,* you say? Perhaps. *Cherry* or *Peach Jubilee* are also very popular. But to these eyes, a blue flame swirling softly over the top of a *Baked Alaska* looks best, what with the lightly-browned Meringue as its becoming background. The "how" lies in countersinking empty eggshell halves in the top of the Meringue before browning it. Then when the Meringue is browned, pour Cognac into the warm shells. Ignite; watch; enjoy.

BAKED ALASKA
(*10 large servings*)

Since Mr. Young has a bountiful supply of quality Ice Cream constantly on hand, and a natural culinary aptitude, perhaps no layman has had more practice in perfecting the Baked Alaska than he. This is his recipe:

> 1 plain White Cake, 9″ square or round, at least 1½″ to 2″ thick
>
> 1 pint each Chocolate, Strawberry, Vanilla, Pistachio (or green Creme de Menthe) Ice Cream and Purple Raspberry Sherbet

Place the Cake on a breadboard covered with brown paper (or on a cookie sheet insulated with 3 layers of aluminum foil). Top the Cake with a 1″-thick layer of each of the five kinds of Ice Cream in the order listed above. Keep well frozen until serving time.

Make a Meringue by beating the whites of 12 large Eggs until very stiff and gradually adding 2 tablespoons Sugar and ¼ teaspoon Salt. Carefully frost the entire sides and top of the Cake and Ice Cream. Sprinkle the Meringue generously with Powdered Sugar. Bake 1 or 2 minutes in a preheated 400° F. oven. Slip the Baked Alaska off the paper or aluminum foil onto a tray or large platter. Pour 1 cup warm (about 100°) Cognac over the Baked Alaska, and touch a lighted match to it. Slice and serve while flaming.

CORIANDER
(Herb and Seed)

Many a gay candy sucker—or hard candy ball—begins as a Coriander Seed. Sugar-coated Coriander Seed are a tasty confection in themselves; "Comfits," the English call them.

Coriander Seed can give an incomparable accent, a soft one, to *Cream Cheese.* The seed, ground or crushed, of this Parsley-family annual from Southern Europe, French Morocco, Argentina, and India, are also taste-tempting in—

Candies, Cakes, Cookies, Danish Pastries, Gingerbread, Biscuits and other *Breads* (this is a popular use of the seed in Europe);
Lentils, Peas, Legume Soups, Spanish Rice, Italian Polenta; French Dressing, Green Salads;
Tapioca Cream, Bread or *Rice Puddings;*
Stewed Apples, Pears, Peaches;
Relishes, Sweet Pickles, Sauerkraut;
Fish, Meat Balls or *Loaf, Beef Stews, Roast Pork, Ham, Mutton, Meat Stuffings* (especially for *Game* or *Poultry*), *Curried Meats, Meat Sauces, Gravies.*

Fresh Coriander leaves may be used much as the seeds are but should be used more sparingly. Incidentally, fresh Coriander Seed have an unpleasant odor and flavor that belie their future culinary potential. In fact, the Greeks named the seed after a bad-smelling little bug called "Coris."

Coriander root was prized as a vegetable by the ancient

Chinese, who also liked the seeds in pastries and drinks and the leaves in soups and salads. Manna, the Bible tells us, was "white like Coriander Seed." Charlemagne (742-814) had Coriander grown in his gardens. This ancient seasoning, which was known in 5,000 B.C., was recommended by Pliny as an antidote against painful scorpion bites. (Perhaps the wine in which the seeds were mixed also helped.)

A pleasant way to get better acquainted with these rich-in-Vitamin-C seeds, which taste like a blend of Sage and Lemon, is to put a teaspoonful of them in your next *Apple Pie* right along with the usual Nutmeg and Cinnamon. Serve hot.

Magicians use the gimmick of burning Coriander Seeds. This produces hallucinations, says an old legend. (Coriander incense was once thought to rout evil spirits.) The pleasure you'll get from a crushed Coriander Seed in your after-dinner coffee will be no hallucination—and it may bring you your true love.

My Favorite CORIANDER SEED Recipe

CRUMB-TOPPED APPLE PIE

Fill an unbaked chilled pastry shell with diced, pared, tart Apples. Sprinkle with 1 tablespoon Lemon Juice, ¾ cup Sugar, and ¾ teaspon Crushed or Ground Coriander Seed. Mix the following topping and sprinkle over Apples:

¾ cup Sugar	½ cup sifted all-purpose Flour
½ teaspoon Cinnamon	½ teaspoon Baking Powder
¼ teaspoon Nutmeg	⅛ teaspoon Salt

1 Egg

Dribble ⅓ cup Melted Shortening over Crumb Topping. Bake 10 minutes at 400° F., and then reduce heat to 350°, and bake 30 minutes longer or until Apples are tender. Garnish each slice of Pie with Whipped Cream topped with a tiny dot of Red Jelly.

COSTMARY
(Herb)

The English once used Costmary's peppery lemonlike flavor to enliven their *Ales*. Costmary *Tea* is still a popular herb tea and tonic.

Charlemagne's Imperial Gardens were graced by this herb that is a native of Western Asia. Ancient cook books made mention of this plant. The Colonists, who transplanted it to the New World, used Costmary's broad leaves as bookmarks in their Bibles, so the herb became known as Bibleplant.

In cookery, a tiny fresh or dried leaf of this aster-family perennial is winning witchery in:

Roast Beef, Grilled Hamburgers, Venison, Wild Duck, Chicken; Pound Cake; Jellies; Teas.

This is another strong seasoning, so begin with only one leaf in the bottom of the roasting or the cake pan until you are well acquainted with Costmary's strength.

❦❦❦

CRACKLINGS

❦❦❦

Pork Cracklings have one popular culinary use—that of season-ing *Corn Bread* (which then becomes *Cracklin' Bread*).

The crisp, dry meat rinds and particles are obtained by slowly cooking (rendering) the fat from the rinds and fatty tissue of Pork.

Cracklings, whose popularity was once limited to the South, are now packaged commercially and marketed nationally as a snack to go with cold beverages. The best kind for Cracklin' Bread are the rich country-style canned by rural women, but it's quite a race to get the Cracklings into jars before the children consume the last crusty morsel.

CRACKLIN' BREAD

Sift together 2 cups Yellow Corn Meal, 1 teaspoon Soda, 1 teaspoon Salt, 1 teaspoon Sugar. Add to the dry ingredients 1 slightly beaten Egg, 2 cups Buttermilk or Sour Milk, ¾ cup finely-crushed Country Cracklings. (If Cracklings are very dry add 1 tablespoon Bacon Fat.) Beat until smooth. Put 1 tablespoon Bacon Fat in a sizzling-hot skillet, and quickly sprinkle 1 teaspoon Corn Meal into the Fat. Pour in batter. Bake 25 minutes at 500° F.

CUMIN SEED or COMINO
(Seed)

❦❧

Roasted Peacock seasoned with Cumin Seed was a kingly dish in mediaeval times. Today several million pounds of Cumin Seed come annually from Iran, French Morocco, Iraq, Turkey, and Syria to make a taste adventure of:

Game, Poultry, Fish, Stews, Meat Loaf, Chili, Tamales, Tamale Pie;

Breads (especially), *Sugar Cookies, Fruit Pies* (use ¼ teaspoon Cumin Seed to a pie);

Appetizers, Stuffed Eggs, Cheese Spreads (the seed are often sprinkled on top for both a garnish and a seasoning); *Soups, Sauces, Gravies;*

Cabbage; Rice Dishes (especially); *Dried Beans, Peas, Lentils.*

The slightly bitter flavor of these dried fruit of a Parsley-family plant, originally from Egypt, is greatly prized in *Spanish, Mexican,* and *Italian dishes,* and also in Oriental meat cookery. *Sauerkraut* seasoned with Cumin Seed is a German idea. German cooks often substitute Cumin Seed for Caraway Seed, for the two look and taste somewhat alike. Cumin Seed are sometimes boiled and mashed before being used in cookery.

Although Ground Cumin Seed is in Chili Powders, many Mexican cooks make particularly delicious *Chili* by adding a teaspoon more Cumin Seed per pound of meat used in Chili con Carne. Combined with Coriander, Cumin Seed are also

used to season *Sausages* and *Cottage Cheese*. These seed are also
an important ingredient of Curry Powder.

". . . ye pay tithe of Mint and Anise and Cummin . . ." said
Jesus in Matthew 23:23. The Romans used this yellow-brown
seed as a Pepper substitute.

Cumin, an annual herb (also one mentioned by Pliny), grows
easily in the garden.

Cumin Seed, long popular with commercial packers of meats,
cheeses, and pickles, is now popular with the home cook, who
first became aware of their excellence in Mexico's national dish.
Now she knows Cumin Seed can bring culinary pleasure to
much other cookery.

My Favorite CUMIN SEED Recipe

CUMIN CHICKEN SALAD

2 cups chopped Chicken (bite
   size)
¾ cup finely chopped Celery
1 teaspoon Onion Juice
⅛ teaspoon Cayenne

¼ teaspoon Crushed or Ground
   Cumin Seed
½ teaspoon Salt
¼ cup Almonds, blanched and
   slivered

1 cup Mayonnaise

Combine ingredients gently in order not to break up Chicken.
Serve in Tomato Roses. Garnish with Mayonnaise and a Pimiento-
Stuffed Olive.

❧❀❧

CURRY POWDER
(Blend)

❧❀❧

This Tiffany of kitchen jewels is most becoming to *Broiled Pineapple Slices* to accompany *Shrimp.* Repeat for *Broiled Tomatoes* to go with any *meat.*

An exotic concoction of some sixteen spices, this seasoning was introduced from India. Although the formula may vary with the manufacturer, Curry Powder usually contains Cinnamon, Mustard Seed, Fenugreek, Cardamom Seed, Turmeric, Garlic, Black and Red Pepper, Ginger, Curry Leaves, Caraway Seed, Cumin Seed, Coriander Seed, Sage, Cloves, Onion, and Salt.

Almost any *Veal, Egg, Rice, Chicken, Fish,* or *Shrimp Dish* can be "Curried" successfully, as well as many *Beef Dishes.* Curried Meat, incidentally, is always accompanied by Rice and Chutney. *Creamed Vegetables* (especially *Cabbage*) are frequently seasoned with Curry Powder.

But the new user should go slowly with this cosmopolitan culinarian until her taste for it is determined—or developed. One-half to one teaspoon in a dish for four is a conservative beginning, but Curry Powder may be mild, rather hot, or very hot, so learn *your* Curry Powder packer.

A spicy start for the new Curry user is a wee touch of the powder in *Cranberry Sauce* to go with Roast Chicken, a bit in *Baked Fish,* a light dusting on the broiling *Lamb Chops,* a dash in the *French Dressing,* a teaspoon of it in the flour for coating *Fried Chicken,* or just a speck in *Cream of Mushroom, Chicken,* or *Tomato Soup.*

Curry Powder has also been pleasantly recognized in: *Chicken Salad* and *Chicken Croquettes, Tomato Juice, Consommé, Oyster Stew, Shrimp Salad, Kidney Stew, Grilled Hamburgers, Creamed Dried Beef, Mushrooms, Cream Cheese Spreads,* and *Toasted Potato Chips.* But most surprising of all was the flavor in a salad of *Sliced Bananas* and *Water Cress.* Recommendation passed. Now, consider *Curried Avocado Dip.* It's worth it.

This Oriental seasoning, which is often called "Salt of the Orient," is internationally popular. In India, where it originated, the Curry blend varies from meal to meal, depending on the disposition of the cook, for she mixes her own Curry Powder to suit her mood and taste. A true Indian blend, however, is usually pungently hot.

Here's how to enjoy this seasoning with a minimum of effort: Cream a stick of Butter or Margarine, and blend ½ teaspoon Curry Powder into it, along with a bit of Cayenne and Paprika. Use this flavored spread for *Sandwiches* (instead of the usual mayonnaise), on *Broiled Meats,* and over *Hot Cauliflower, Broccoli, Carrots,* and *Peas.* And don't forget it on *Toasted Crackers* to go with the soup or the salad.

For an after-show snack, Curry-seasoned *Scrambled Eggs* will close the evening on a high note.

Left-over *Meat* can make a worthy *pièce de résistance* when renovated with Curry Sauce.

My Favorite CURRY POWDER Recipe

CURRY-MUSHROOM SAUCE

Blend ⅓ cup Milk into a can of Condensed Cream of Mushroom Soup. Add 1 tablespoon Curry Powder. Heat thoroughly.

This sauce is delicious over Open-Faced Chicken Sandwiches, Rice to go with Broiled Chicken, or Chopped Meat.

DILL
(Herb and Seed)

Although Dill grows easily in almost any garden, much is imported from India. The fresh or dried leaves, seed, or Dill Salt can give an unsurpassed flavor to:

Apple Pie; Tomato Juice, Avocado Dip, Cottage or *Cream Cheese;*

Potato Salad, Cole Slaw, Macaroni Salads, Green or *Vegetable Salads, Fish Salads, Sour Cream Dressings;*

Butter for Sandwiches or for Seasoning Broiling Meats;

Beets, Carrots, Cucumbers, Cabbage, Squash, Cauliflower, Turnips, Potatoes, Green Beans, Sauerkraut, Tomatoes;

Pork or *Lamb Chops, Boiled Beef, Creamed Chicken, Veal Dishes, Gravies;*

Fish, Shrimp, Lobster (Dill in Drawn Butter to go with these is something!), *Fish Sauces;*

Bean or *Tomato Soup, Borscht; Egg Dishes.*

Pumpkin cooked as a vegetable is improved by a bit of freshly minced Dill (and Onion). Meat packers value Dill Seed, which are available whole or ground, for seasoning *Liverwurst, Bologna,* and *Frankfurters.* Tan Dill Seed, which have a faint Caraway tang, can substitute for Caraway Seed—even in sweet foods. Dill Seed were chewed as a delicacy by the Colonists, often to keep themselves awake during long sermons. Today we often nibble Dill Seed thoughtfully in *Cream Cheese Canapés* while meditating on party chatter that evidently was never intended to be complete.

Roman and Greek heroes were crowned with this Parsley-family annual, which Virgil labeled, "A pleasant and fragrant plant."

Dill Pickles like a lot of this herb, but other cookery calls for a light touch of it, but *do* let Dill out of the pickle jar. This pleasant herb can glamorize many of our dishes.

―――――――――――――――――――――――
My Favorite DILL SEED Recipe
―――――――――――――――――――――――

DILLY COOKIES

2 Eggs, beaten light
1 cup Sugar
1 cup Cream (heavy)

1 tablespoon Baking Powder
3 cups sifted all-purpose Flour
1 teaspoon Salt

1 tablespoon crushed Dill Seed

Add Sugar slowly to the well-beaten Eggs. Add Cream, and mix well. Sift Baking Powder and Salt with Flour, and then mix in Dill Seed. Combine all ingredients. Chill dough four hours. Then roll dough and cut with cookie cutter. Bake cookies at 350° F. until lightly browned.

DITTANY
(Herb)

Dittany's pleasantly aromatical leaves are used in *Green Salads* and also in many other ways much as fresh Marjoram leaves are. Ditty can also go in to relieve Chervil. The flavor of Dittany, a member of the Mint family, is especially compatible with *Fruit Flavors*. Dittany's pretty pink flowers are for ornamental use, not culinary.

DURKEE'S FAMOUS DRESSING

Deviled Eggs were my downfall until a good-cook friend told me to use this unique dressing for seasoning them. (Although the word "unique" is more often misused than not it does apply to this condiment, for I know of no similar product on the market.) And don't you agree *Stuffed Eggs* are difficult to season well? So good when well seasoned, so uninteresting when not.

For an unusual *Slaw Dressing,* blend together two parts of this Dressing with one part Whipped Cream, and add ½ teaspoon Celery Seed.

Potato Salad is another food that's difficult to season satisfactorily, but not with this Dressing; the Sauce's light penetrating flavor goes right through the cold Boiled Potatoes. (Potato Salad is always better if made a day in advance of serving.)

Whipped Potatoes are superlative when a big spoonful of this creamy Sauce is blended into them. The same treatment gives a fillip to *Cream Gravy* to go with Fried Chicken.

One of the best things about this Sauce, of course, is that it's just right "as is" for topping *Head Lettuce Salad, Cold Broccoli, Asparagus Spears,* or *Tomato Slices*—also *Broiled Fish* and *Meats.*

Used as a seasoning, this Sauce gives the flavor of a gourmet medley of spices and herbs that never hits a sour note, not even when used by an inexperienced hand.

My Favorite DURKEE'S FAMOUS DRESSING Recipe

ASPARAGUS MERINGUE

Fill a greased casserole half-full of drained cut Asparagus Spears. Pour over the Asparagus a rich sauce made as follows:

Stir 3 tablespoons Flour into 3 tablespoons Melted Margarine or Chicken Fat. Stir in slowly 1½ cups hot Milk. Cook over low heat, stirring constantly until sauce is thickened. Then add slowly the well-beaten yolks of 3 Eggs. Mix well. Add ⅛ teaspoon each Celery and Onion Salt, ½ teaspoon Dry Mustard, ⅛ teaspoon Cayenne, 2 tablespoons Durkee's Famous Dressing.

Make a Meringue (unsweetened, of course) of the 3 Egg Whites, and fold into the stiffly-beaten Egg Whites 3 tablespoons Durkee's Famous Dressing. Spoon the Meringue over the Asparagus. Bake 15 to 20 minutes at 300° F., or until thoroughly hot and the Meringue lightly browned.

FENNEL or SWEET FENNEL
(Herb)

❦❦❦

He who eats Fennel will enjoy clear vision, says an old legend that is mentioned by Shakespeare. The cook who flavors her *Apple Pie* with Fennel Seed (which look and smell much like exaggerated Anise Seed) will certainly enjoy more favorable culinary comments.

The sweet-hot, licorice-flavored ground seed of this Celerylike annual of the Parsley family are also used, whole or ground, to lift the taste quality of:

Lentils, Green Vegetables, Sauerkraut; Candies; Spiced Peaches; Beef, Lamb, Pork; Cod, Halibut, Shellfish, Boiled Fish, Fish Sauces; Salad Dressings; Breads, Pastries, Puddings; Beverages; Egg or *Cheese Dishes.*

Fresh Fennel leaves are used in *Soups, Fish, Puddings,* and *Salads.* Latin countries serve young Fennel stalks (often called "Italian Celery") as a *Salad Green* and also much as we serve Celery. The enlarged leaf base is often cooked as a vegetable.

Fennel's flavor and fragrance, suggestive of Anise, are popular in Swedish and Italian cookery. Italian bakers prize Fennel Seed on *Breads,* and Scandinavians use them in many *Baked Products;* the affinity is between Baked Flour and the seed, of course.

Fennel, like Dill sprigs and also Bay Leaves, was used in ancient times to crown Roman heroes. Our forefathers nibbled the seed at church, so Fennel (like Caraway and Dill Seed) became known as "meetin' seed." Wise men of old considered Fennel, which was one of the first herbs used in cookery, to be one of the nine sacred herbs that were thought to counteract the nine causes of diseases.

Greek mythology tells that knowledge of Fennel came to man as a coal of fire in a stalk of Fennel—directly from Mount Olympus. Today most of our Fennel comes from India, France, Lebanon, and Argentina.

My Favorite FENNEL SEED Recipe

CRUSTY LOAVES

1 cake or envelope Yeast	6 cups sifted all-purpose Flour
2 cups lukewarm Water	2 tablespoons Whole Fennel
1 tablespoon Salt	Seed

1 Egg White

Dissolve the Yeast thoroughly in the Water. Add the Salt. Add Flour slowly, mixing well.

Knead dough for 15 minutes on a lightly-floured board. Place dough in greased bowl, cover, and let rise 2 hours, or until double in size. Punch dough down, and knead another 5 minutes. Divide dough into two equal portions, cover well, and let rest 12 minutes. Shape the dough into pointed loaves.

Sprinkle cookie or baking sheet lightly with Corn Meal. Place loaves on the sheet. Let rise about 1 hour, or until double in size. Brush the tops of the loaves with the slightly beaten Egg White, and sprinkle generously with Fennel Seed. Bake 10 minutes at 425° F., and then lower heat to 350°, and bake the loaves an hour longer.

❧§❧

FENUGREEK or FOENUGREEK
(Seed)

❧§❧

These seed give the "maple" flavor to many *Candies*.

The aromatic seed of this annual pea-family herb, the only leguminous herb, are imported from India, France, Lebanon, and Argentina, although the plant is native to Southern Europe.

In ancient Egypt a fever remedy was made of Fenugreek Seed by soaking them in water until they swelled to form a thick paste.

The yellow-brown seed, which are pleasantly bitter with a flavor that reminds one of caramelized sugar, are an ingredient of Curry Powder. *Chutney,* that dark fruity relish that accompanies Curried Meats, is flavored with Fenugreek Seed.

※❀❀❀※

FINE HERBS (FINES HERBES)
(Combination)

※❀❀❀※

This term means finely minced herbs for seasoning *Sauces, Soups, Green Salads, Gravies, Stews, Omelets, Broiled Steaks,* and many other foods. (The French term *les fines herbes* refers to Sweet Basil, Chervil, Sweet Marjoram, Thyme, Rosemary, and Tarragon.)

A Fine Herbs Combination might include:

Parsley, Chives, and Chervil; or Burnet, Parsley, and Thyme; or Chives, Basil, and Parsley.

A combination recommended especially for *Pork Dishes* is Sage, Savory, and Basil. Tarragon was once included in Fine Herbs, but since its flavor tends to dominate it slipped from grace for this use (but don't underestimate Tarragon).

Fine Herbs become an integral part of the food in which they are blended, while a "bouquet" (see BOUQUET GARNI) is usually removed before the food is served.

(Lemon Juice will do Garlic hands that are perfumed from the fresh cloves.)

To season cooking food with Garlic, pierce a clove with a toothpick, and drop it into the food. Remove the clove before serving the food. Leave the clove in longer for a stronger taste. Subtle flavor could rub the serving bowl or salad bowl with a cut clove, but that hardly rated. For a milder taste to toss a crust of bread that has been rubbed in Garlic, salad (Chapon) with the

❦❧

GARLIC
(Herb)

❦❧

Handled discreetly Garlic can make any cook famous, just as it has many foreign chefs (especially Italian and French). The Garlic gamut runs from simple *Salads* through marvelous *Meats*.

The novice's first taste of Garlic may call to mind strong sprouted Onions, but experience with it will soon make Garlic's own robust flavor highly distinctive and entirely different to that of Onions. (Don't shy away from combining the two seasonings.) Once a taste for Garlic is developed there is no satisfactory substitute for this vegetable.

This historic annual of the lily family, which grows the world over, was prized by the ancient Chinese and also the Greeks. The bulbs, which are divided into cloves, were used as a vegetable by Egyptian slaves. (Although Garlic is a vegetable, it is usually referred to as an "herb.") Some Garlic enthusiasts today rave over a *Sandwich* made of Sweet Butter, slivered Garlic, and lots of Parsley. Charlemagne had Garlic grown in lavish quantities.

Garlic is still prized today for giving an epicurean touch to:

Steaks, Pot Roasts, Meat Loaf, Spaghetti Meat Sauce, Lamb; Green Beans, Broccoli, Spinach, Tomatoes; Seafood or Green Salads; Breads; Cheese Dishes; Soups (especially *Tomato*); *Vinegars.*

In addition to the fresh bulb form, Garlic is available as a salt, powder, oil, or liquid. Garlic Salt, which is fresh-flavored, is popular in American kitchens. No Garlic-ed fingers from it.

(Lemon Juice will de-Garlic hands that are perfumed from the fresh cloves.)

To season cooking food with Garlic, pierce a clove with a toothpick, and drop it into the food. Remove the clove before serving the food. Same tactics for French Dressing. For use in Salads, many cooks rub the wooden salad bowl with a cut clove, but that limits *that* bowl. French cooks like to toss a crust of bread that has been rubbed with a cut clove (*chapon*) with the salad. The *chapon* is usually removed before the food is served, but it won't be fatal if forgotten.

For Garlic bread, put a clove of Garlic through a Garlic press, a helpful little gadget that costs a silver dollar, directly into Creamed Butter or Margarine. (For a not-hard-to-clean press, leave the skin on the clove, but be sure to point the root end of the clove down.) After spreading Bread Slices with it, stack them back in loaf form, and tie. (When using French Bread, don't cut the slices quite through the bottom crust.) Place the tied loaf in a paper bag, and close the end with a paper clip. Heat the Bread thoroughly in a hot oven, and serve promptly.

Never brown a clove of Garlic! Sauté it, yes, but browning too much gives Garlic a flavor that belongs in no food.

Publicity concerning cooking with Garlic reached such dizzy heights a few years ago someone retaliated with "How NOT to Cook With Garlic!" But good cooks will always cook with Garlic.

My Favorite GARLIC POWDER Recipe

EGG-TOMATO CASSEROLE

6 hard-boiled Eggs
1 dozen Soda Crackers
½ cup grated Sharp Cheddar
3 large Tomatoes
2 tablespoons Butter or Margarine

1¼ cups Chicken Broth (or 1 Chicken Bouillon Cube dissolved in Hot Water)
⅛ teaspoon Garlic Powder
⅛ teaspoon Black Pepper
Salt to taste

Arrange the sliced hard-boiled Eggs and Tomato Slices in alternate layers in a greased casserole. Roll Crackers fine, and pour hot Chicken Broth with seasonings over two-thirds of them. Add half the Butter to the Crumbs, and beat well. Stir in the Cheese. Pour mixture over Eggs and Tomatoes in casserole. Sprinkle remaining Crumbs on top, and dot with remaining Butter or Margarine. Bake about 20 minutes at 420° F. Serve with Broiled Bacon.

My Favorite GARLIC SALT Recipe

GARLIC CHICKEN

"This dish is so popular that many of my friends have adopted it for their own," said Olive Sykes, Society Editor of *The Lakeland Ledger* of Lakeland, Florida, when she gave me this recipe which she developed. I have certainly adopted it, for it is the easiest, tastiest method of preparing Chicken with which I am familiar.

Wash and cut a frying-size Chicken as for frying. Melt ½ stick Butter or Margarine in a casserole in the oven. Salt and Pepper the Chicken. Dip the pieces into the melted Shortening so all sides are coated, letting Chicken remain in the casserole. Sprinkle generously with Garlic Salt. Bake uncovered in a 450° F. oven. Just before Chicken is browned nicely, pour over it 1 can of Sliced Mushrooms, and continue cooking Chicken until well browned.

❧❦❧

GINGER
(Spice)

❧❦❧

Forget *Gingerbread* momentarily. Dribble melted Butter over golden *Grapefruit Halves,* sweeten them with Honey, and then spice them with a flurry of Ginger. Broil. Serve for breakfast, or as an appetizer or dessert for lunch or dinner. Then you'll agree a pinch of this tantalizing spice is still worth as much as a pound of it once was (16 ounces or so would purchase a mutton in the Tenth Century).

Buff-colored Powdered Ginger can also make taste triumphs of:

Pie Pastry (for any kind of pie), *Cookies, Spice Cakes, Pumpkin Pie, Pineapple Upsidedown Cake; Bean* or *Potato Soup;*

Applesauce, Pear Dishes (Ginger always "goes with" Pears), *Bananas, Stewed Peaches* or *Prunes;*

Pot Roasts, Broiled Steaks, Pork Chops, Meat Loaf, Lamb, Veal, Fried or *Broiled Chicken* (rub pieces of Chicken with Ginger, and then cook as usual), *Sugar-Cured Hams;*

Mayonnaise, French Dressing (especially for *Fruit Salads*);

Custard-Type Desserts (including *Tapioca*), *Indian Pudding; Carrots, Cauliflower, Creamed Onions, Baked Beans.*

Powdered Ginger is widely used in Oriental cookery. This ingredient of Curry Powder is also used in great quantities by meat packers—and *Grilled Cheese Sandwich* enthusiasts.

"Cracked" Ginger is small pieces of unground Ginger Root; it is used to season *Chutney, Pickles, Stewed Fruit, Preserves,* and *Conserves.* White Ginger is the scraped peeled roots.

Candied or Crystallized Ginger (often called Canton Ginger) is sometimes prepared in Honey, instead of Sugar; this type of Ginger is a confection and tea tidbit, not a seasoning. Nevertheless, use it to make a sparkling sensation of *Baked Puddings, Fruit Desserts, Whipped Cream* for topping desserts, and tiny hot buttered *Biscuits* for tea.

Ginger roots, or "hands," come from a perennial grown in British West Africa, Asia, Jamaica (the best comes from here), India, Cuba, and China. Incidentally, when Marco Polo's travels were published in the early 1300's, his account of having seen Ginger growing in China helped start the competitive search for a sea route to the Orient.

Crushed *Ginger Snaps* mixed into *Cream Cheese* for topping *Bartlett Pears* on Endive make a snappy Salad that always attracts pleasant attention. (Six or so Ginger Snaps can also be used to thicken and flavor *Brown Gravy;* just crumble them in instead of using Flour.)

The ancients used *Ginger Tea* to soothe an ailing stomach. A pinch of Powdered Ginger does help indigestion. The next time you come home from work in a gingery mood, try relaxing in a hot tub of water perfumed with a teaspoon of Ginger. Leisurely thoughts of rich spice caravans will soon replace Twentieth Century pressures. (It was to members of a spice caravan that Joseph of the Multi-Colored Coat was sold by his jealous brothers centuries before Christ.)

In Old England, Ginger was often sprinkled on *Ale* or *Porter,* which was then stirred with a red-hot poker to heat the drink. *Ginger Beer,* long popular on the Continent, has now come into favor in America where *Ginger Ale* has long been a favorite. Have you tried this effervescence over *Fruit Cups?* Ginger Ale Cubes appear at the best parties, often with a Mint Leaf or a Cherry frozen in the center of each cube.

Ginger Sour, that famous cooling drink, is made by mixing 5 tablespoons Ginger, 1 cup Vinegar, ¾ cup Lemon Juice, 2 cups

Sugar, and 2 quarts Ice Water. Serve over Ice Cubes. Garnish with a merry Maraschino.

A Horse's Neck is a long glass of Ginger Ale chuckfull of Ice Cubes, sporting a long, long curl of Lemon Peel (peel of the entire Lemon is cut spirally); one end of the Peel nuzzles the glass's rim. Its excuse for being is to keep the teetotaler from being conspicuous, but neither he nor the drink needs one.

Raisin-eyed Gingerbread Men are still the favorite but short-lived companions of the young fry.

My Favorite CRACKED GINGER Recipe

PEAR PRESERVES

Pare, core, and slice thinly not-too-ripe Pears. Use an equal amount of Sugar as of prepared Fruit. Pour Sugar over Fruit, and let stand overnight. (This toughens Pears, giving them a chewy texture.) Pour into a heavy, shallow pan, and place in a 400° F. oven. As soon as Fruit begins to boil, reduce heat as low as possible. Stir Fruit occasionally while cooking. When Sirup thickens slightly, place Preserves in jars, with a piece of Cracked Ginger in each jar, and seal.

This may be prepared on top the stove, of course, but must be stirred much more frequently.

My Favorite GROUND GINGER Recipe

GINGER REFRIGERATOR COOKIES

1 cup Butter or Margarine	½ cup Molasses
1 cup Sugar	1 tablespoon Ground Ginger
2 Eggs, well beaten	1 teaspoon Soda
4½ cups sifted all-purpose Flour	1 teaspoon Salt

Cream Shortening, and add Sugar gradually. Add Eggs and Molasses. Sift dry ingredients together, and add, mixing well. Shape into a roll, and wrap in waxed paper. Chill several hours. Slice very thin, and bake 10 to 12 minutes at 400° F.

GRENADINE SIRUP

This thick scarlet Sirup is usually made from Pomegranates but sometimes from Red Currants. Grenadine Sirup, which is non-alcoholic, is used to sweeten and flavor *Beverages* (especially *Cocktails*); *Fruit Cups, Salads,* and *Compotes*; and is also used as a *Sauce* for *Puddings* and other *Desserts*.

Four tablespoons of Grenadine Sirup added to the usual French Dressing recipe, along with a bit of grated Lemon Peel, makes an engaging *Dressing* for *Fruit Salad*.

My Favorite GRENADINE SIRUP Recipe

WHIPPED HONEY DRESSING

Beat 1 pint Strained Honey on high speed 10 minutes. Add gradually 2 tablespoons Grenadine Sirup and ⅛ teaspoon Salt. Serve on any *Fruit* or *Melon Salad*.

GUMBO FILÉ

Without Filé Powder—and Okra—there would be no *Gumbos*.

Although this is one of the most limited in use of all food seasonings, it is indispensable to *Gumbos*. Filé Powder is made up primarily of dried, ground leaves of the American Sassafras tree but may also contain Thyme or other herbs.

If boiled this seasoning turns dark green and becomes thick and slippery, so it should be added only after the *Gumbo* is cooked and has stopped boiling. How much? One teaspoon to each quart of *Crab, Shrimp, Oyster,* or *Chicken Gumbo*.

Filé, which is like nothing else you've ever tasted, enjoys warm popularity in Creole cookery. (*Gumbos* are Creole, of course.) But the Sassafras idea originated with the Choctaw Indians.

My Favorite GUMBO FILE Recipe

FILÉ SPREAD

Here's a Filé fun food for cocktail party use:

Cream a stick of Butter or Margarine, and blend into it 1 tablespoon Filé, a teaspoon of Paprika, and a few drops of Lemon Juice. Spread on Crackers. Garnish each with a tiny Shrimp that has rolled gaily in finely-minced Parsley.

HOREHOUND
(Herb)

Horehound stick candy and drops were the delight of Nineteenth and early Twentieth Century youngsters. This oddly bitter confection is still available in some drug stores. And *Honey-Horehound Candy* is currently staging a comeback.

Flavoring Extract is made from the leaves of this perennial of the Mint family that now grows as a weed, for use in *candies* and *liquors*. The plant's fresh leaves were once popular in *Herb Tea. Horehound Honey* is another good *Honey.*

The Greeks and the Romans were familiar with Horehound's healing qualities for lung and throat ailments. The herb is still used as a cold remedy today. In the Ozark Mountains the leaves are simmered in water to cover for many hours (sometimes days); the essence is then drained off and further concentrated by more boiling. But even with added honey it's still a bitter dose.

The flowers and the tender sprigs of Horehound are still used in *Meat Sauces, Pastries, Cakes, Homemade Candies,* and *Beef Stew.*

HORSERADISH
(Herb)

Mouth-burning, nose-tickling, eye-stinging Horseradish has been popular as a food seasoning for thousands of years; it is known the world over.

The most popular use for the grated root of this perennial of the Mustard family, which is often mixed with Vinegar or Whipped Cream (sweet or sour), is as a condiment to go with *Roast, Boiled,* or *Corned Beef; Mutton; Oysters, Shrimp,* or other *Seafood;* and *Pork Chops.*

Applesauce laced with this masterful flavor and served as Ham's companion will make you glad you *did* buy that big Ham. Young leaves of the large Horseradish plant are used in *Green Salads* and also as *Cooked Greens.*

Prepared Horseradish is available bottled in Vinegar or dehydrated. When using freshly grated Horseradish, blend it with Lemon Juice rather than the usual Wine Vinegar. It's better. Horseradish *Butter* wins by a whole length over other spreads for Sandwiches. Men especially shout the praises of Horseradish's hearty flavor on *Beef-on-Rye Sandwiches.*

A bit of this peppery seasoning in the *Cream Cheese Canapés* makes guests ask flattering questions. (And most accomplished cooks enjoy giving out their "secrets.")

My Favorite HORSERADISH Recipe

CHEESE DIP FOR POTATO CHIPS

Beat until smooth 2 3-ounce packages Cream Cheese. Add slowly
1 tablespoon Cream, 1½ tablespoons Mayonnaise, ⅛ teaspoon Onion
Powder, 1 teaspoon Worcestershire Sauce, 1 tablespoon Prepared
Horseradish, and 4 tablespoons very finely minced Dried Beef.
Hollow out the center of a pretty Red or Green Cabbage, and fill the
Cabbage with the Cheese Mixture. Place on tray, and surround the
Cabbage with large Potato Chips.

HYSSOP
(Herb)

Hyssop's sweet-scented flowers give the world one of its finest honeys.

In Sicily a sprig of Hyssop is often hung in homes to keep bad luck away.

This blue-flowered perennial of the Mint family has prestige among the herbs used in repentance and purification ceremonies. Many Biblical references are made to it; David sang of Hyssop.

For culinary use the minty, slightly bitter leaves of this plant, when used with a delicate hand, can bless:

Soups and *Broth; Candies; Stews, Game* and other *Meats; Fat Fish; Vegetables; Fruit Cups, Punch, Pies,* and *Gelatins; Cranberry Relish.*

❦

JUNIPER BERRIES

❦

These warm, pungent-tasting, berrylike fruits have an especial affinity with *Veal*. (They give *Gin* its characteristic flavor.) The berries can also give individuality to *Lamb, Mutton, Ham, Beef,* and any *Meat Stew*. The Germans like this seasoning in *Sauerkraut*.

Sportsmen praise Juniper Berries for taming the flavor of *Wild Duck, Grouse, Pheasant, Goose, Quail, Rabbit, Venison,* and for improving *Stuffings, Marinades,* and *Sauces* for all game.

This strong-flavored seasoning must be used cautiously—five or six berries to the roasting pan, four or five in the stew.

You can harvest your own Juniper Berries in late October and dry them for year-round use. Or pickle them in scalding Cider Vinegar, salted to taste. Seal the bottles tightly and store in a cool, dark place for a few weeks before using. A bit of this bittersweet Vinegar will improve *Game Marinade*.

My Favorite JUNIPER BERRY Recipe

WILD DUCK

After removing feathers from Duck, dip the down-covered Duck into a large container of Hot Water in which 1 or 2 cakes of Paraffin have been melted. (The Paraffin stays on top the Water and coats the Duck as it is brought up from under the water.) Let cool a few minutes. Then use a dull table knife to scrape the caked Paraffin and down from Duck.

Dry Duck, and rub well inside and out with Flavor Salt. Place inside Duck 3 Juniper Berries, 1 Onion, 1 small Carrot. Seal Duck air-tight in aluminum foil. Place on a cookie sheet and bake 25 minutes at 500° F. Then unwrap foil over Duck's breast, and brown it quickly under broiler.

This Duck is wonderfully juicy, but not too rare for the average palate. The juices may be served as they come from pan, or they may be thickened. (Avoid using as much of the Duck Fat as possible, for it is strong-flavored.)

LARDOONS
(Pork)

This musical-sounding word means homely little strips of Fat Pork, about one-quarter inch thick and of any convenient length, that are used to lard *Lean Cuts* of *Meat,* especially *Beef.* Frequently Lardoons are rolled in a fragrant mixture of Pepper, Nutmeg, Allspice, etc., before being inserted in meat. (This is the case with Tennessee's *Spiced Round of Beef,* a traditional Christmas meat.)

A larding needle, which is a hollow metal tube, is used to insert the Lardoons into the meat being larded. The needles are a specialty item, available only at better kitchenware stores; a sharp-pointed knife can substitute very well. A luscious Lardoon is inserted in the eye of the needle, and the pointed end is then pushed through the meat.

Larding is not difficult, and it makes meat juicy and succulent. When the larded meat is carved, the white bits of Pork give it an attractive studded appearance. Incidentally, the term "larding" may also mean just laying strips of Salt Pork or Bacon over the breast of a fowl or on cuts of meat.

LAVENDER
(Herb)

Although this perennial is primarily sachet-popular its flower petals are also used occasionally to give an exotic flavor to:

Fruit Punches, Jellies, Lemonade, Wine Cups.

Lavender's fresh flowers are used to garnish summer beverages. Lavender honey is another of the fine honeys.

LEEK
(Herb)

"The poor man's asparagus," French peasants call these tasty plants, which are available only in our larger markets. Leeks are often boiled, baked, or braised much as Celery is. To prepare Boiled Leeks, wash and trim the vegetables and cook in boiling, salted water until tender. Then drain the Leeks and serve with plenty of Melted Butter or Margarine and Paprika. (It's difficult to get all the grit out of these plants. Best to quarter them lengthwise and then wash them well under much running water.)

This floral emblem of Wales, which has been prized as a seasoning since the days of the ancient Egyptians, is strongsmelling but mild Onion-flavored. The Leek resembles the Onion in appearance but is larger, and in flavor it's sweeter.

These plants are used, whole or in part, to make epicurean experiences of *Green Salads* and *Soups,* especially *Vichyssoise.* Nero was especially fond of *Leek Soup.*

My Favorite LEEK Recipe

LEEK SALAD

Simmer the white part of Leeks in Chicken Stock only until tender. Drain, chill, and serve on Water Cress with French Dressing. Garnish with a full-blown Radish Rose.

LEMON

When all else fails to give that extra something to a food call in tart, tangy Lemon Juice. But don't wait for that emergency. Start with tonight's *Hamburgers*. Blend this benefactor into the Ground Meat before shaping into patties.

Salad Dressings like a fifty-fifty billing between Vinegar and Lemon Juice, as do those elegantly rich little *Chess Tarts* which the South esteems. Desserts prompt the thought of *Hot Lemon Sauce*. Do you know how quickly it can be made from Frozen Lemonade Concentrate? Just heat and thicken the Concentrate with a bit of Cornstarch and enrich with that traditional lump of Butter size of a Walnut, and a speck of Nutmeg. *Good* on *Bread Pudding* or *Vanilla Ice Cream*.

A Salt-free dieter declares his strict diet has been worth the discovery of Lemon's legerdemain on *Hot Vegetables, Cold Asparagus Spears, Tomato Slices, Green Salads,* and over *Meats.* Also use Lemon Juice in or on:

Soups (*Consommé needs it*); *Cakes, Pies; Fruit* or *Vegetable Juices; Stewed Fruits; Fish, Shellfish; Steaks, Pork Chops, Chicken, Liver* and *Roasts.*

Broiled Fish of the best quality still comes up lacking when not showered with droplets of this Citrus Juice. *Black Bean Soup* sparkles when a few gratings of Lemon Peel fall into it. And *Chicken* likes a Lemon rub-down before being broiled, baked, or fried. One steak house we patronize showers its *T-Bones* with Lemon Juice before broiling them.

Lemon Juice Concentrate is good for all-round culinary use, but not if you've got a Fresh Lemon on hand. (You'll always have one if you use the trick of storing Lemons in a covered jar in the refrigerator.)

Best way to have grated Lemon Peel on hand is to settle down and grate a quantity at one sitting and freeze it in little aluminum foil envelopes, or just seal it tightly in little jars in the refrigerator (the grated Peel will keep several days).

Keep Golden Lemon, the most royal and loyal of all food fixers, at work, for it can add flavor appeal to both sweet and nonsweet foods.

My Favorite LEMON JUICE Recipe

LEMON SAUCE FOR VEGETABLES OR MEATS

Cream 1 stick Sweet Butter, and add to it ½ teaspoon Celery Salt, ⅛ teaspoon White Pepper, and 1 teaspoon Parsley Flakes (or a tablespoon of freshly minced). When the ingredients are well mixed, stir in slowly 1½ tablespoons Fresh or Bottled Lemon Juice. (If Salted Butter or Margarine is used, omit Salt.)

LEMON VERBENA

Dried Lemon-scented Verbena leaves are delightful in sachets, of course, although their fragrance evaporates with the passing months. For culinary use, the tender green leaves can add a dainty elegance to: *Fruit Salads, Punch, Wine Cups, Custard Puddings, and Jellies.*

Tea is brewed from the dried leaves.

As a finger bowl or fruit cup *Garnish,* a fresh leaf of Lemon Verbena is a fragrant addition.

My Favorite LEMON VERBENA Recipe

CUSTARD SAUCE FOR PUDDINGS

Beat 4 Egg Yolks slightly, and add to them ¼ cup Sugar and ⅛ teaspoon Salt. Stir in slowly 2 cups Scalded Milk. Cook over hot (not boiling) water, stirring constantly, until the Custard will coat a silver spoon. Remove from heat promptly. (Should the Custard curdle from too much heat, beat with a rotary beater to restore the Custard's smooth texture.) Add 1 teaspoon Vanilla.

Pour the Custard over 3 or 4 Lemon Verbena leaves in a jar, and let cool. Refrigerate promptly when cool.

✥

LOVAGE
(Herb)

✥

French cooks revere Lovage which has the fresh fragrance and flavor of Celery but is much stronger; however, Lovage may be used in any way Celery is. (When substituting Lovage for Celery, use only half as much Lovage as you would use of Celery.) To be more specific, the tender leaves are used, fresh or dried, to give a Celery flavor to:

Stews, Sauces, Soups; Fish and *Fish Chowders; Green Salads; Marinades; Teas.*

The stems of Lovage (another of the herbs an Irish monk taught Charlemagne about) are used much as Angelica is, both for flavoring and decorating *confections*. The fresh leaves are cooked as Greens; the stalks are cooked much as Celery is.

Lovage Seed are used in *Candies, Pastries, Game, Meats,* and *Fruit Salads*. (The oil from the seed is used in medicines.) The seed are an especially desirable addition to *Mutton, Braised Pork,* and *Beef Stew*. Incidentally, Lovage Seed make an interesting substitute for Celery Seed (Lovage Seed are a little sweeter than Celery Seed).

This tropical-looking perennial, which was once widely cultivated in gardens for use as a home remedy *Tea,* can be grown from either seed or root divisions.

My Favorite LOVAGE SEED Recipe

LOVAGE PECAN BALLS

1 cup Butter or Margarine	2 cups Pecans, chopped fine
½ cup Confectioner's Sugar	2 teaspoons Lovage Seed
⅛ teaspoon Salt	(Whole)
2 cups sifted all-purpose Flour	2 teaspoons Vanilla

Cream Shortening until very light, and gradually add Sugar. Add Flour, Salt, Nuts, Lovage Seed, and Vanilla. Roll dough into small balls, and place on an ungreased cookie sheet. Press top of each ball lightly with tines of fork. Bake at 350° F. 15 minutes or until firm and lightly browned. Remove and roll in Confectioner's Sugar while the Balls are hot.

❧❧❧

MACE
(Spice)

❧❧❧

Two pounds of the "Pound Cake Spice" would buy a cow in the Middle Ages. Today one-fourth teaspoon of it in *Cherry Pie* makes it seem as valuable as of old.

Although Mace's aroma and flavor are much like those of Nutmeg, there is a difference. Mace is more delicate.

Whipped Cream can be improved—with Mace. One teaspoon Mace to a pint of Whipped Cream makes the rich Cream much less oily-tasting and more flavorful. Mace can also improve:

Spinach, Cauliflower, Carrots, Succotash; Fish and *Fish Sauces; Chocolate Desserts, Custard Puddings, Custard Sauces, Doughnuts, Yellow Cakes, Gingerbread; Sausage, Meat Loaf, Veal Chops, Hogshead Cheese, Gravies, Stuffings; Tomato Juice; Stewed Fruits, Fruit Salads; Oyster Stew, Consommé, Cream Soups; Pickles, Preserves, Jellies; Cheese Dishes* (especially *Welsh Rarebit*).

And Mace is enchanting in *Macaroni* and *Cheese*—or *Mashed Potatoes.*

This spice appears in most blends of Pie Spices, Poultry Seasonings, Meat Seasonings, and Sausage Seasonings. Whole Mace, called "blades," are found in Pickling Spice and are often used to flavor *Jellies* and *Stewed Fruits.* (Mace is sachet-popular, too.)

Mace is still a relatively expensive spice because of the difficulty of preparing it. It is the red lacy network that encloses the Nutmeg, which network, by the way, turns orange as it dries. (Nutmeg is the seed of a small pear-shaped fruit.) Mace and Nutmeg, the only two spices to come from one and the same tree, are interchangeable in cookery.

When the Dutch were in strict control of the spice trade in the Seventeenth Century and Mace brought a better price than Nutmeg, the Amsterdam merchants sent instructions to the Spice Islands to destroy half the Nutmeg trees and to plant more Mace trees! Pigeons helped outwit these same merchants who were trying to restrict the Nutmeg tree to the Spice Islands (now the Moluccas). The birds liked the bright red Mace that peeped through the Nutmeg fruit, and often flew to other islands to eat the Mace from the Nutmeg they were carrying. There the pigeons dropped the Nutmeg, and it grew and flourished.

Today most Mace (and Nutmeg) comes from Indonesia and the West Indies.

(Also see NUTMEG.)

My Favorite MACE Recipe

POPOVERS THAT POP

Break 2 Eggs into a bowl. Add 1 cup sifted all-purpose Flour, ½ teaspoon Salt, ½ teaspoon Mace, and 1 cup Milk.

Mix with a fork lightly only until Eggs are blended. Don't worry about the small lumps. Pour batter into 6 well-greased *glass custard cups* (cold ones) on a cookie sheet. Place in cold oven, and turn temperature gage to 450° F. Bake 30 minutes without peeking even once. Then turn off heat.

Take the Popovers from the oven and remove from the custard cups. Puncture tops to let steam escape. Place on cookie sheet and return Popovers to oven to dry 10 minutes. Serve promptly with lots of Butter or Margarine and Jam.

(This recipe has never failed me.)

MARGARINE

The French, those culinary masters, whipped up the first Margarine in the early 1800's—and it's been popular in Europe ever since.

But Margarine's impact on the American home cook is best described by the wail of a farmer's wife: "I've got ten pounds of Butter I can't sell at 50c a pound. People have gotten used to Margarine and *like* it!"

Yes, Margarine *is* here to stay: the improved flavor, long-keeping qualities (you can buy a month's supply in advance), the smooth texture and positive vitamin enrichment process assure it. Added assurance that Margarine is not transient comes from its fresh, delicate flavor—the result of quality ingredients, cottonseed and soybean oils blended with a mixture of pasteurized skim milk, salt and coloring, produced with a carefully controlled manufacturing standard.

And Margarine is just as nutritious and digestible as Butter. The fat content of Margarine and Butter are the same—80% by weight, and Margarine's vitamin content is uniform the year 'round.

Margarine is easy to spread and easy to blend, too, and is more spatter- and stick-proof when used for frying . . . and not the least important, Margarine costs, usually, less than half the price of Butter!

Most cooks' reluctance to accept Margarine wholeheartedly when it first came on the American market (it's been popular in Europe for decades) was based on its white, unpalatable appearance—and also on the necessity for working coloring (which came in powdered or liquid form in an envelope or capsule) into Margarine by hand. (There were few, if any, home mixers in those early Margarine days.) Now, however, because of popular insistence, yellow Margarine is available in all but two of the forty-eight states. So, today, more cooks use Margarine than Butter, both in cooking and on the table.

Like Butter, Margarine is boxed in four quarter-pound sticks or "prints." Thoughtful Margarine manufacturers now pack Margarine in "measure sticks," so the housewife can quickly cut off as many tablespoons as she may need, thus eliminating a greasy measuring cup.

Wonder who will get on the market first—the dairymen or the Margarine men—with an herb-flavored fat? Many more cooks would use herbs and spices for seasoning *Vegetables, Broiled Meats,* and *Sandwiches* were such a spread available. (For the home cook, it's an untidy job to soften Margarine or Butter and then whip it and blend in the spices. Too often, she just doesn't get around to doing it.) We're betting on the Margarine manufacturers, for their research chemists have long been geared to a hard, fast pace in putting more flavor into Margarine. Who knows, perhaps even next year we'll be able to buy a pound of Margarine containing four sticks of different flavors—Chives, Parsley, Garlic, and Cinnamon!

Margarine, backed up with other seasonings, *can* give double-portion appeal to our dishes.

My Favorite MARGARINE Recipe

PINEAPPLE REFRIGERATOR CAKE

Cream ½ cup (1 stick) Margarine. Add slowly 1½ cups Sugar, creaming mixture thoroughly. Then beat in 2 eggs, 1 at a time. Add

⅛ teaspoon ground Cardamom Seed, 1 cup *drained* (juice will cause the mixture to have a curdled appearance) Crushed Pineapple, and 1 cup finely-chopped Pecans.

Line a loaf pan with aluminum foil. Place it in alternate layers of Vanilla Wafers and the creamed mixture, ending with Wafers on top. Use 1 pound of Vanilla Wafers in all. Cover with aluminum foil, and place 2 bricks (or other heavy weight) on top of cake. Let ripen in refrigerator 24 hours before serving. Then slice and serve garnished with Whipped Cream, Cherry, and Mint Sprig.

This dessert, which has no raw-egg flavor whatever, is especially easy and good-tasting. It keeps well for several days.

❧❧❧

MARIGOLD

❧❧❧

The fresh or dried petals of this garden flower can give both flavor and flair to:

Salads; Braised Beef, Pot Roasts, Game, Stews; Chowders, Chicken Soup, Broths; Custard Puddings (place 2 fresh petals in bottom of baking dish); *Cakes, Cookies, Buns; Beverages.*

French and English cooks like to use Marigold, fresh or pulverized, and this seasoning is the golden secret of much good Dutch cookery (as it was of mediaeval cooks who flavored and colored their *Soups* with this flower).

Marigold is a good substitute for expensive Saffron, but get acquainted with the flavor before venturing beyond one or two petals. An easy beginning can be made by placing them in the bottom of the pan in which the *Yellow Cake* is to be baked.

ᵉᵍᵉ

MARINADES

ᵉᵍᵉ

The magic of a Marinade is comparable to that of Wine; in fact, Wine is often used as a Marinade. (See WINE.) The magic is simply this: A Marinade gives both flavor and tenderness to *Meats*.

One of the most popular Marinades is made by combining:

⅓ cup Vinegar
⅓ cup Salad Oil
⅓ cup Broth, Vegetable Stock, Mirepoix, etc.
   Spices to taste (these often include Bay Leaf,
      Peppercorns, Red Pepper, Whole Allspice,
      Juniper Berries, Whole Cloves).

The mixture is then poured over Meat which is allowed to stand overnight in the refrigerator, or at least for several hours. The Meat is turned occasionally to let the Marinade penetrate it. The Meat is then drained and braised, baked, broiled, or pot roasted as usual, depending on the cut and the cook.

Many sportsmen insist on their *Venison, Duck, Bear,* and other *Game* being marinaded prior to cooking. Those famous German dishes *Hasenpfeffer* and *Sauerbraten* are prepared in Marinades.

Boiled Crab or *Shrimp* for cocktails or salads are improved by being marinaded in French Dressing a few hours prior to serving. *Boiled Chicken* for salads, à la King, etc., is tastier if marinaded in a White Wine or Sherry to give it Wine's intriguing flavor and aroma.

ఴఴ

MARJORAM or SWEET MARJORAM
(Herb)

ఴఴ

Marjoram's bitter undertone is a prime favorite in *Veal Cutlets*, especially when backed up by Savory. (It is best to pound the herbs into meat with the edge of a saucer.)

Lima Beans, Green Beans and *Peas, Tomato Juice, Potato Dishes, Liver,* and *Dumplings* are also especially superior when graced with Marjoram's flavor, but many foods frequently invite this herb to the dinner table:

Poultry, Game, Pork, Beef, Meat Loaf, Sausage, Meat Balls, Stews, Veal Roast, Hash, Brains, Lamb, Mutton, Duck, Turkey, Swiss Steak, and any *Meat Stuffing* at all;

Broccoli, Brussels Sprouts, Eggplant, Carrots, Spinach, Zucchini, Asparagus, Onions, Cole Slaw, Mushroom Dishes (always!), *Green Peas;*

Omelets; Rarebits; Cheese Straws, Balls, and *Soufflés;*

Trout, Salmon, and *Salmon Croquettes; Baked Fish, Tuna Fish, Creamed Crab;*

Salads of *Cottage Cheese, Fruit, Green Peppers, Tossed Greens,* or *Vegetables;*

Madrilene; Chicken Noodle, Turtle, Clam, Oyster, and *Onion Soups.*

"*Wurstkraut*," the sausage herb, the Germans call this seasoning, although its grey-green leaves are adaptable to *any Meat* or *Vegetable Dish.* The leaves are available either whole or grou

The best of this strong, sweetly-fragrant annual of the Mint family comes from France, Germany, and Chile, but Marjoram is at ease in the home garden— and the *Salad Bowl*. Shakespeare agreed: "We may pick a thousand salads ere we light on such another herb." And one of Shakespeare's heroines was complimented by being called, "The Sweet Marjoram of the salad bowl."

The *Punch Cup* is glamorized by a fresh Marjoram leaf—as also is a *Fruit Salad* by several. A few freshly-minced green leaves blended into *Cream Cheese* for Orange Bread Sandwiches at tea time will be popular as greenback.

There are Sweet, Pot, and Wild Marjorams, but Sweet is that usually found growing in gardens, for it has the most delicate flavor of the three, making it best suited for culinary use.

Marjoram, which combines especially well with Thyme, predominates in many Poultry Seasonings. *Bologna, Liverwurst, Headcheese,* and many other processed Meats boast this aromatic seasoning.

Latin cooks are devoted to fresh Wild Marjoram (Oregano is its dried form) for seasoning *Lamb, Fowl, Stuffings,* and *Fresh Mushrooms,* but it is available at only a few foreign shops. *Pizza Pie* popularity called our national attention to Oregano, which is on most spice counters now. (See OREGANO.)

Like Basil, Marjoram is held sacred in India. (Basil also teams well with Marjoram for seasoning *Veal.*) Queen Bess is said to have preferred perfumes that contained Marjoram's stimulating fragrance.

In ancient Rome and Greece, Marjoram was a symbol of happiness; newly-married couples were crowned with it. Today, used lightly, Marjoram still bespeaks happiness—in the pleasures of the table.

My Favorite MARJORAM Recipe

FRIED ASPARAGUS

Dip short Asparagus Stalks in fine Bread Crumbs seasoned with Marjoram (½ teaspoon Marjoram to 2 cups Crumbs), Salt and Pepper. Then dip into a beaten Egg that has been diluted with 1 tablespoon Cold Water, and then back in Crumbs again. Let dry a few minutes, and then fry in deep hot fat.

(These will stay crisp some minutes if serving is delayed.)

MAYONNAISE

Although Mayonnaise is not usually looked upon as a food seasoning, it can be a delightful one.

A spoonful of Mayonnaise in *Creamed* or *Boiled Potatoes* seems even better than Butter as an occasional change (probably the piquancy of the Vinegar).

Mayonnaise can give both eye- and palate-richness to *Hot Green Vegetables*. The use of Mayonnaise in *Salads* would call for its own book! (And for that use Mayonnaise is more than a seasoning, of course; it's a basic ingredient.)

This Dressing makes the daintiest and tastiest *Breakfast Toast* that has ever come from my oven. Spread Bread Slices thinly but evenly with Mayonnaise, and brown them lightly under the broiler. (It's fun to spring this one as a surprise.) In fact, this is "My Favorite Recipe" using Mayonnaise as a seasoning.

(See CHERVIL for a *Hot Vegetable Sauce* recipe that is made with Mayonnaise.)

MEAT DRIPPINGS

Use for making *Gravy,* yes, but the concentrated liquid and fat left in the roasting pan where Meat has been cooked also has other uses. (There's usually much more than enough for basting during cooking and making gravy.)

After removing the cooked Meat and taking out enough drippings for immediate Gravy-making, pour a little scalding water into the crusted pan. Then scrape loose all the brown sediment with a wooden spoon. Pour the mixture into a bowl, and let cool until the fat has solidified on top. Remove cake of fat to another container. The fat can be used for seasoning *Vegetables* (especially *Browned Potatoes*) and in making *Corn Bread.* Use the flavor-rich broth (which should be stored in a covered jar in the refrigerator) as a base for additional *Gravy,* and for *Sauces, Chili, Stews,* and *Soups.*

If Meat Drippings seem inclined to scorch during the cooking of Meat, add a bit of water to the pan and lower the heat, for scorched Drippings *are* scorched Drippings.

The Drippings from the Breakfast Bacon should be cooled and stored in a jar in the refrigerator. The experienced cook knows what they can do for *Green Beans, Baked Beans, Corn Bread,* and *Scrambled Eggs.* The same cook knows that *good* Bacon Drippings come only from Bacon that has not been cooked too quickly.

❧❦❧

MEAT TENDERIZER

❧❦❧

Although a marvel in itself, a Meat Tenderizer is not always a food seasoning, but we have a choice between Unseasoned and Seasoned Tenderizers. Many cooks want both kinds on hand— the plain to use on cuts of Meat which she prefers to season with her own imagination and spices, the seasoned type to use when in doubt or in a rush.

Tenderizers are one of cookery's greatest boons. In them, home cooks can have—for a few cents—a secret that was long limited to famous chefs.

MINCEMEAT SPICE
(Blend)

This artful blend of Cloves, Allspice, Cinnamon, etc., is used to spice the *Mincemeat,* of course, but it is also a fragrant mystery in *Cookies, Pudding Sauces,* and *Cakes.* It's interesting to use Mincemeat Spice in *Sweet Rolls* occasionally as a change from Cinnamon. (Never let the name of a spice blend hamper you; the name is intended to start a chain of thought . . . "If Mincemeat Spice is good in *Mincemeat* that means it's also good in *Raisin Pie, Spice Cakes* and *Cookies, Sweet Pickle Relishes,* and—." See?)

My Favorite MINCEMEAT SPICE Recipe

CANDIED APRICOTS

Boil together 5 minutes 1 cup Water and 2 cups Sugar. Remove from heat. Drop Dried Apricots into the Sirup and remove them promptly to drain on waxed paper or a cake rack. Roll each Apricot in Granulated Sugar that has been sifted with Mincemeat Spice (1 teaspoon to 1 cup Sugar). Let dry thoroughly, and then store in air-tight tins.

Children especially like these easy confections, although these sweets are interesting enough for party use.

MINT
(Herb)

Have you tried crushing Mints and folding them into *Whipped Cream* for topping Chocolate Desserts? Or "frosting" a cake with Chocolate Mints? (Simply lay the Mint Patties on the warm cake, and a moment later spread them gently with a spatula.)

Mint's tangy sweet flavor has a cool aftertaste that makes it delightful in—

> *Cheese Spreads* for hors-d'oeuvres;
> *Teas, Punch, Fruit Juices, Vinegars;*
> *Jellies, Sherbets, Ice Cream, Chocolate Desserts* (sensational!);
> *Potatoes, Peas, Carrots, Green Beans, Spinach;*
> *Fruit Cups, Applesauce, Fruit Salads;*
> *Tossed Salads, Cole Slaws;*
> *Soups* (especially *Pea* or *Bean*);
> *Fish* and *Meat Sauces* (especially for *Lamb* or *Veal*).

Although Mint Sauce on *Lamb* is traditional, a thoughtful hostess queries her guests before ladling the Sauce directly on the Meat.

A sprinkling of freshly-minced Mint Leaves can give a charming change to the usual *Tomato Salad.* And since you're probably waiting for it, we'll just mention it: Kentucky's famous *Mint Julep.*

Candied Mint Leaves are an appealing garnish for *Fruit Salads, Tea,* and *Desserts.* Small tins of the delicacies make hits as gifts with gourmet friends. (Just brush the fresh clean leaves with Egg White and then sprinkle well with finely granulated Sugar. Let dry thoroughly before storing between layers of waxed paper in air-tight tins.)

There are Curly Leaf Mint, Peppermint, Apple Mint, Orange Mint, Pineapple Mint, Pennyroyal (which often enhances *Wine Cups*), and Spearmint. Frosty-flavored Spearmint is the most popular for culinary use. Dehydrated Spearmint Flakes, which are a quick seasoning for *Sauces* and *Soups,* are available at spice counters. Peppermint is more generally used in Candies and Medicines.

Although Mint originally came from Europe and Asia, we now grow most of our own. Mint makes a fragrant house plant—one that stands ready to garnish *Desserts* and *Drinks.*

Mint is found growing wild on many a shady creek bank. A rooted plant, transplanted to a damp, shaded spot—perhaps by the bird bath or the water hydrant (Mint *must* have lots of water)—will spread quickly into a bed. The bed area should be hemmed in with brick or boards to keep this gadabout plant at home. Pinching the tops out of the plants occasionally will make them bushy and keep them from going to seed. Although fresh Mint is better in flavor than dried, this herb, like others, can be dried on screens or simply be hung in loose bunches to dry in a dark, cool place.

A tiny vase of fresh Mint sprigs gives a cool fragrance to a room. The gimmick is to crush two or three leaves and drop them inside the vase before arranging the sprigs. The Greeks and the Romans appreciated Mint's refreshing fragrance so much they often used Mint to improve the air in their banquet halls. Today, we appreciate Mint most of all in a tall glass of *Iced Tea.*

Hostesses often tuck sprigs of this refreshing plant in the centerpiece on the dining room table.

Mint Extract is a satisfactory substitute for flavor, but not for flourish.

My Favorite MINT LEAVES Recipe

MINTED BAKED APPLES

Wash and core 5 or 6 Rome Beauty Apples, and peel upper fourth of each Apple (this helps Apples keep their shape). Place a few Mint Leaves or Flakes in the bottom of a casserole, and place Apples on top the Leaves. Fill center of each Apple with 2 tablespoons Honey, 1 Mint Leaf, ¼ teaspoon Butter or Margarine, and 1 teaspoon Water. Cook covered at 375° F. until almost tender. Then remove cover, baste Apples with Sirup from baking dish, and finish cooking uncovered.

❦❦❦

MIREPOIX
(Vegetable Stock)

❦❦❦

This first-rate seasoning is of our own concocting. Make it daily by simmering those bits of Vegetables that a not-in-the-know cook might let end up in the garbage can. Such things as:

Onion Peels, Garlic Clove Trimmings, Leek Trimmings, Turnip Peelings, Water Cress and Parsley Stems, Celery Tops, Green Pepper Trimmings (even the biting seeds are good for this use), Rutabaga Peelings, Carrot Scrapings, Tomato Tops.

Don't overlook *anything*—except:

Mushy greens, like Spinach or Broccoli; strong-flavored vegetables, like Cabbage; starchy vegetables, like Corn or Potatoes (they scorch too easily).

After simmering the Vegetables in water to cover until tender, strain out and discard the Vegetables. Cool and refrigerate the Stock.

Use Mirepoix to add flavorful vitamins to *Stews, Gravies, Soups,* and *Sauces.* (Many famous French Sauces depend on this Stock.) Also use it to substitute for water in *Vegetable Cookery,* and as a flavor-rich *Basting* for Roasting Meats, and as a *Marinade* ingredient. But use this sorcerous Stock as promptly as possible, or freeze it in small, not-quite-full jars.

❧❧❧

MONOSODIUM GLUTAMATE
(Chemical)

❧❧❧

MSG must have sent many a copywriter down in defeat. It *is* difficult to give a chemical a personality, but the character of this contemporary "condiment" has already earned the Crystals a permanent niche in our spice cabinets.

Unless you had chemistry, don't bother trying to figure out the "how" of these 99% pure Monosodium Glutamate Crystals. Just accept them on faith. Even though they are not a true condiment, flavoring, or seasoning, they "do something" to food. This chefing-aid, which adds no flavor of its own, brings out the full *natural* flavors of *Meats, Fish, Poultry, Gravies, Stuffings, Sauces, Vegetables, Soups, Salads,* and *Creamed Dishes*—whether the basic ingredients are fresh, frozen, or canned.

MSG, which is made from amino acid and glutamic acid (both of which occur naturally in all vegetable and animal protein), is marketed under many different brand names (Accent, Zest, Enhance, Praise-Allah Seasoning, etc.), but "Monosodium Glutamate" appears on each of the labels. Some MSG's, such as Enhance and Praise-Allah Seasoning, are herb-flavored.

Your tasting-spoon baton can make sweet dinner music directing these proportions (which are correct for all brands) of MSG:

Appetizers: Use ¼ teaspoon Crystals to each cup *Cheese* or *Meat Spread*.

Meats: For *Broiled, Roasted, Fried,* or *Sautéed Meats,* rub ½ teaspoon Crystals per pound of Meat into the *Meat* before cooking. For *Breaded Fish, Cutlets,* etc., mix 1 teaspoon Crystals with each half-cup fine Crumbs for breading the Meat.

For *Ragôuts, Stews, Chili, Meat Sauce* for *Spaghetti, Chop Suey,* and other such Meat dishes, add ½ teaspoon Crystals to each pint hot cooked food, and blend well.

Sauces, Gravies and Creamed Dishes: Use ½ teaspoon Crystals to each cup Sauce for *Creamed Fish, Seafood, Chicken, Cheese, Vegetables, Macaroni,* etc.

Soups: Blend ½ teaspoon Crystals into each pint cooked liquid.

Eggs: For *Creamed, Deviled, Curried, Scrambled,* or *Fried Eggs,* use ⅛ teaspoon Crystals per *Egg.*

Salads: Use ¼ teaspoon Crystals to each cup of *Salad (Egg, Chicken, Meat, Green,* or *Seafood).* For *Tossed Green Salads,* add the Crystals to the Greens before mixing the dressing into them.

Vegetables: Use ¼ teaspoon Crystals to each cup *Fresh, Frozen,* or *Canned Vegetables* (except Potatoes) before cooking.

For *Scalloped, Au Gratin,* or *Mashed Potatoes,* use ½ teaspoon Crystals to each pound of Potatoes. For *Fried or Hashed Brown Potatoes,* use the same amount as for other Potatoes, but add Crystals to Potatoes before cooking.

The best cook we know, Miss Wilma, declares, "MSG is an excellent toner-upper."

❧❧❧

MUSHROOM SAUCE
(Condiment)

❧❧❧

"Every cook commends his own sauce," must have been said originally of the clever cook who first concocted Mushroom Sauce.

Although this "steak" sauce, which is made of dried Mushrooms, Malt, Soy Sauce, Salt, and Spices known only unto the maker, is popularly classed with the other good meat sauces, this one can give a singularly pleasing flavor to: *Egg Dishes; Meat Dishes,* such as *Stews, Ragôuts; Sauces, Gravies.*

Also, when used as a *basting* the sauce adds an excellent accent to *Broiling* or *Roasting Meats.*

Mushroom Sauce will always be dashed with light abandon on *Lamb Chops* and *Steaks.* The good cook also dashes the sauce into any meat dish at all to make *that* dish.

❦❦❦

MUSHROOMS

❦❦❦

Mushrooms are everyday Truffles.

Although these aristocratic beauties are a food in their own right, we also use them to give added richness, savor, and interesting texture contrast to other foods. In fact, Mushrooms can make impressive fare of many everyday foods.

Mushrooms can't be misused, but for those cooks who haven't gotten around to considering these delicacies, they're used especially in *Creamed Meat* or *Vegetable* or *Poultry Dishes*. Rich-tasting Mushrooms also combine well with *Hot Green Vegetables*. Add sliced Mushrooms to the *Butter Sauce* or *Cream Sauce* to go over any meat or poultry. Broil them whole for garnishing *Steaks*.

Tough, woody stems don't go in the garbage can, but in the soup pot, for everything about a Mushroom is good.

Mushroom Butter can accentuate the goodness of a *Filet Mignon. Canapés* coated with the spread are indescribably good.

Peeled, sliced raw Mushrooms add something to the *Tossed Salad*.

Mushroom Sauce (thin a can of Condensed Cream of Mushroom Soup with ⅓ cup Milk, and season to taste) is one of the cook's best face- and menu-savers in times of unexpected guests. The *Sauce* is festive over *Fried Chicken, Open-Face Ham Sandwiches, Croquettes, Rice*—as you already know. But have you used this Sauce in making *Scalloped Potatoes?* Good, isn't it?

One of the broadest planks in my cookery campaign is the *Mushroom Omelet*. I promise it will please.

MUSTARD
(Herb and Seed)

❧❧❧

Once upon a time there was a little blond girl named Doris Lee who daily insisted on Prepared Mustard on her Raisin Cookies, although she was chided, "Mustard doesn't go with sweet things." The gentle bite of Mustard in today's *Fruit Salad Dressing* is an affirmation of that child's native good taste.

Mustard's bite is even sharper, more enjoyable, on a *Steak* that has been rubbed with Olive Oil and Dry Mustard before broiling. And who ever heard of a *Ham Sandwich* without Mustard, either Dry or Prepared?

Light or dark Mustard Seed (two varieties) are used whole or ground to give a spark to:

Baked Beans, Creamed Onions, Beets, Succotash, Cabbage, Lima Beans;

Salad Dressings, Cole Slaw, Cocktail and *Barbecue Sauces;*

Newburg or *Cheese Sauce* (½ teaspoon to each 2 cups *Sauce*), *Welsh Rarebit; Egg Salad, Creamed Eggs; Cream Soup;*

Pickles, Relishes;

Creamed or *Broiled Seafood, Deviled Crab;*

Chicken, Turkey, Roast Beef, Game, Ham, Sausage, Roast Pork.

Potato or *Fish Salads* call for a generous amount of this peppy powder that casserole cookery finds indispensable.

Mustard Seed are grown widely in Canada, The Netherlands, Italy, Denmark, Europe, the Orient, and also in California and Montana. Mustard Flour (Dry Mustard) was first used in cookery by the English in 1720, when a housewife ground and marketed Mustard Seed powder.

Mustard's sharp, pungent flavor is delightful mixed with those of other spices and Vinegar to make Prepared Mustard, long popular on *Cold Cuts, Hot Dogs, Hamburgers, Ham Sandwiches,* and in *Gravies.* There are several types of Prepared Mustards, best known of which are Bahamian (spicy and hot), French or Dijon (spicily pungent), English(pure sharp Mustard flavor), and Holland (another spicy Mustard).

Some herb-scented golden Mustards are sandwich-worthy in themselves. The most popular herbs for flavoring Prepared Mustard are Basil, Horseradish, Lovage, Marjoram, Oregano, Parsley, Rosemary, Sage, Tarragon, and Thyme.

The father of modern Medicine, Hippocrates, praised Mustard for its healing qualities. That Mustard plaster treatment for respiratory ailments *is* old-fashioned—it's been used for centuries. A Mustard-perfumed bath is said to help a cold.

Mustard Seed were processed in Roman-occupied Britain by saturating them in a grape juice solution called "must," so the seed became known as "must seeds," and then finally as Mustard. Jesus mentioned this ancient spice (Matthew 17:20): "If ye have faith as a grain of mustard seed, ye shall say unto this mountain, remove hence . . ."

Tender young Mustard Leaves are used as a *Salad Green* and also as *Cooked Greens.* Mustard has been enjoyed both as a seasoning and as greens since the days of ancient Greece. Mustard was quite popular in Old English cookery. (Shakespeare referred to this herb.) That Mustard will always be popular in cookery is a safe prediction.

My Favorite DRY MUSTARD Recipe

BAKED PORK AND BEANS

1 tablespoon Dry Mustard

2 teaspoons Onion Flakes

2 strips Bacon, finely chopped

⅛ teaspoon Black Pepper

3 tablespoons Honey (or Brown Sugar)

1 teaspoon Worcestershire Sauce

Open 2 cans Pork & Beans into a bowl, and season with the above. Pour into a well-greased casserole, and bake 10 minutes at 450° F. Reduce heat to 300°, and bake 1 hour. Then lay bits of more chopped Bacon over top, and dribble another tablespoon of Honey lightly over top of Beans. Bake another hour, or until Bacon on top is crisp and the top well glazed.

These Beans are delicious hot or cold. They're especially good with Barbecued Beef, Pork, or Lamb.

My Favorite MUSTARD SEED Recipe

MUSTARD SEED PICKLE

Wash and slice thinly 2 dozen unpared 4″ Cucumbers. Sprinkle with ½ cup Salt, and let stand 2½ hours. Drain. Add 3 thinly-sliced Onions. Mix the following ingredients, and pour them over the Pickles:

1 cup Mustard Seed

1 tablespoon Celery Seed

1 teaspoon Fennel Seed

4 cups mild Vinegar

½ cup Virgin Olive Oil

After mixing the Cucumbers and the Seasonings well, place Pickles in jars and cover with lids. Let ripen at least three weeks before using.

Variations of this rich-flavored Pickle recipe have long been culinary classics.

NASTURTIUMS

Nibbling Nasturtium's bright blossoms is an Oriental custom. Americans like the blossoms better as a garnish on *Fruit Salads*.

The green leaves are a "natural" for complementing the flavor of *Meat Spreads* for Sandwiches. This gay flower, which "turns and twists the nose," can also give a fragrant flair to *Tossed Salads* and *Hors-d'Oeuvres Spreads*. (Chop *all* the Nasturtium—flowers, tender stems, and young leaves.)

The yellow-red blossoms, minced and blended into *Creamed Butter* or *Creamed Cheese* for spreading on thin rounds of *Orange-Nut Bread* make delightful Sandwiches. Party favorites. Family tea favorites.

Nasturtium Seed are a deft addition to Pickling Spice. A single seed can be a spicy surprise in the *Tea* cup. To pickle the Seed, pack them while green in small bottles, and add a bit of Tarragon, if you wish, and a Peppercorn or two. Salt Vinegar to taste, and heat to boiling point. Pour Vinegar over the Seed, and seal bottles. Store in a cool, dark place as you would any Pickle. Your "Capers" will be ready to embellish *Salads* and *Dressings* in a month.

Nasturtium Vinegar, which has a wonderful knack with a *Tossed Salad,* was one of our grandmothers' favorites: Fill a jar with full-blown blossoms, and pour cold Wine Vinegar over them. Let stand six weeks. Then dip your tasting spoon in to see if the flavor is right for you. If it isn't strong enough, let the Vinegar stand another week or two. Then strain, bottle, and cork.

NUTMEG
(Spice)

❧❦❧

Sweet, warm, spicy Nutmeg is especially appetizing in *Rice Pudding, Custard Pie, Baked Custard, Bread Puddings, Apple Pie, Applesauce,* and *Cakes.* But have you tried Nutmeg in *Hamburgers?* In *Lemon Pie?*

A tiny particle of this spice can brighten *Black Bean Soup.* Also expect to find Nutmeg in:

Consommé, Beef Soup, Cream Soups;
Broccoli, Cauliflower, Cabbage, Green Peas, Sweet Potatoes, Fried Apples, Creamed or *Soufflé Spinach, Cooked Greens, Succotash;*
Mushroom Sauce, Cream Sauce; Doughnuts;
Scrambled Eggs, Chicken Dishes, Oysters;
Fruit Salad Dressings, Pickles; and in the *Pastry* for *Meat Pies.*

Many cooks prefer to buy Whole Nutmegs and grate them as needed; the flavor's fresher, they say, than that of the ready-ground. An easy test is a grating over a bowl of *Bananas* and *Cream.* (It is true that whole spices retain their flavors longer than ground ones, but aren't the ground ones convenient?)

This spice is the seed of the apricot-like (though pear-shaped) fruit of the Myristica tree of Indonesia and the East Indies, where the natives make the fruit into preserves. Like an Orange tree, the Nutmeg tree may carry blossoms, green fruit, and ripe fruit simultaneously.

The people of Southern Germany traditionally grate Nutmeg

into their *Beer, Flip, Mulled Cider,* and *Hot Punch.* Many German tankards have a ball thumbpiece which serves as a receptacle for the Whole Nutmeg. A grating of Nutmeg makes the drinks both tastier and more digestible. The same goes for Nutmeg on *Whipped Cream.*

During the centuries when Holland monopolized the Nutmeg trade, Nutmegs were soaked in milk-of-lime to destroy their fertility. Even today Nutmegs are sometimes white from lime powder, for it prevents insect attack.

Connecticut is "The Nutmeg State," which sounds like a misnomer, since Nutmeg comes only from the tropics. But sly Yankee traders of bygone days are responsible for the nickname; they passed off wooden Nutmegs that had been drenched in Nutmeg Extract for the real thing. More clever are those people who carve Nutmegs into fragrant miniature trinkets.

Pigeons played a role in making Nutmeg easily available. See MACE for that story. (Mace is the network that covers the Nutmeg.) Nutmeg and Mace can substitute for each other in cookery.

Sweet-smelling Nutmeg was used as a fumigant in the streets of ancient Rome. Today, Nutmeg's wafted fragrance makes one wonder if dinner will *ever* be ready.

Nutmeg works wonder with a cup of creamy *Eggnog*—and it's guaranteed not to put you to sleep as *Nutmeg Tea* was once thought to do. This spice can work even greater magic when a pinch of it is blended into cooking *Spaghetti.* (Many Spaghetti lovers insist on it.) No wonder Nutmegs were once sold as charms, for Nutmeg does bring much charm to cookery.

My Favorite NUTMEG Recipe

NUTMEG SAUCE

Mix in a saucepan 1 cup Sugar, 1 tablespoon Flour, ¼ teaspoon Salt. Stir in 2 cups boiling Water. Cook slowly 5 minutes, stirring frequently. Remove from heat, and add 1 tablespoon Butter or Margarine, 1 tablespoon Sherry, and ½ teaspoon Nutmeg (or more if you like a heavy Nutmeg flavor).

This simple sauce can turn lowly Bread Pudding into a *haute cuisine* creation.

OLIVE OIL

The young cook should be told early about Olive Oil: Buy only the *best* or none at all. And, in this case, high price usually also indicates high quality.

Only Virgin Olive Oil, the delicately-flavored Oil from the first pressing of ripe olives, should be used in cookery. (Oil from the second pressing isn't too bad. but it does have a little stronger flavor.) There are California, Italian, and Spanish Olive Oils, some high quality oils in each type.

Olive Oil may be used in almost all types of cookery, but the Oil is least used in baking. (Oh, perhaps it is drizzled over Pizza Pie, but it is seldom used as the basic shortening in baked products.) Neither is Olive Oil ideal for French-frying foods, for at high temperatures it tends to impart too strong a flavor to foods. (Also, good Olive Oil is much too precious to be used in this quantity.) However, foods are often sautéed in this delectable oil.

French Dressing makes most frequent use of Olive Oil. Three parts Oil to one part Vinegar or Lemon Juice, plus the Seasonings you like, are the standard proportions. Many tossed salad artists prefer to season their creations by dribbling the Oil (and the other Dressing ingredients) directly onto the Greens in the salad bowl.

Mayonnaise made with Olive Oil arouses gastronomic enthusiasm. But too many cooks limit this Oil to salads. Let Olive Oil also help keep you out of food ruts by using a few teaspoons of it occasionally to season *Cooked Vegetables*.

Of all cooks, Italian cooks have the keenest appreciation for this seasoning, even to dribbling its goodness over their enormous *Hard-Roll Sandwiches*. But, then, all good cooks are devoted to Olive Oil.

ONIONS
(Herb)

The versatile Onion is widely used in *Cheese* and *Egg Dishes,*
Shellfish, Meats, all types of *Vegetables, Green Salads, Sauces,*
Soups, Game, Salad Dressings, and in numerous *Combination*
Dishes.

The essence of Onion is available in Salt, Powder, or Liquid
form. Dehydrated Onion Flakes can save many tears; these Flakes
stand ready to garnish *Consommés* or to help in turning out quick
Onion Rolls.

There are a dozen how-not-to-cry-over-peeled-Onion recipes.
The best one is the trick of drowning the juice squirter under
running cold water while tangling with it. For a good cry that
will last a long time, peel and chop a number of Onions at one
time, and freeze them in individual "servings." These call for
prompt cooking after thawing. (They can be dropped unthawed
into the *Stew,* of course.) Get the habit of letting these short-cut
Onions give appetite appeal to *Canned Peas, Green Beans, Corn,*
and other vegetables.

There are three degrees of sautéing Onions for use as a seasoning (cooked Onions are less "Oniony" than raw ones):

1. For a *mild Onion flavor,* sauté sliced or minced Onions in
Butter only until tender. Use these especially to season *Creamed*
Dishes.

2. For a *slightly stronger flavor and a little color,* sauté Onions until lightly browned. Use these in *Soups, Hamburgers,* etc.

3. For a *robust flavor and a rich brown color,* sauté Onions in a lightly-greased skillet until dark brown. Use these to season and color *Stews, Ragôuts,* etc. (This type Onion, which French chefs brown directly on a range plate, can substitute for Caramel as a coloring agent.)

The best Onion for *Salad* use is, of course, the sweet Bermuda; in *Sandwiches,* they're a kingly snack. (Most white Onions are milder than yellow or red ones.)

Young Onions, sometimes called Scallions, have a more delicate, sweeter flavor than mature ones. Scallions are beguiling chopped up in *Green Salads* or used as a seasoning in *Meat Dishes, Fish, Poultry,* and *Egg* or *Cheese Dishes.* Try placing one or two in the cooking *Green Beans* or the *English Peas.* After indulging in these delights raw, chew a sprig of Parsley—or two.

Tiny pickled "Pearl" Onions make tempting hors-d'oeuvres. Two tablespoons of them in *French Dressing* are a culinary crinkle you'll enjoy over a *Green Salad.*

The delicious Onion is one of the best known and oldest of all food seasonings. Its original area isn't known. Both Homer and Pliny wrote of the Onion which is popular the world over. Italian cooks consider the Onion one of the greatest joys of all cookery.

There's only one danger in Onion: Its flavor is so good, so adaptable, we're tempted to put it in every meat or vegetable on the menu. Onion *should* go in every *Green Salad Bowl.*

> "Let Onion atoms dwell within the bowl,
> And, scarce suspected, animate the whole."

> SYDNEY SMITH
> *Recipe for Salad Dressing*

My Favorite ONION FLAKE Recipe

CHOP SUEY

¾ pound Beef, diced
¾ pound Pork, diced
1½ cups chopped Celery
4 tablespoons Onion Flakes
½ Green Pepper, chopped
1 can Bean Sprouts
1 can Mixed Chop Suey Vegetables

1 large can Mushrooms, sliced
¼ cup blanched, slivered Almonds
1½ teaspoons Salt
¼ teaspoon Black Pepper
1 tablespoon Parsley

Fry Beef and Pork in Bacon Drippings until well browned. Add Green Pepper and Celery, and simmer 20 minutes. Add Canned Vegetables and Seasonings, and simmer 45 minutes. Thicken mixture with 3 tablespoons Cornstarch dissolved in 3 tablespoons Cold Water. Cook 5 minutes longer. Add Almonds. Serve over Chow Mein Noodles with Soy Sauce, accompanied by Hard Rolls and a Tossed Salad.

My Favorite ONION POWDER Recipe

PINK SHRIMP

2 pounds Raw Shrimp, shelled and deveined
½ cup Melted Butter or Margarine

¾ teaspoon Salt
⅛ teaspoon Cayenne
½ teaspoon Onion Powder
1 tablespoon Parsley Flakes

2 tablespoons Lemon Juice

Sauté all ingredients, except Lemon Juice, in the Shortening, stirring frequently. When Shrimp begin to curl and turn pink, add Lemon Juice, and cook a moment longer. Test a Shrimp by breaking it. (It should be slightly crisp; shrimp toughen if overcooked.) Serve with Rice, Green Salad, French Bread, and a Fruit Pie.

My Favorite ONION SALT Recipe

MACARONI-CHEESE LOAF

8 ounces Macaroni, cooked with 1 teaspoon Onion Salt in water

1½ cups Milk, scalded

4 tablespoons Butter, melted in the Hot Milk

1 cup soft Bread Crumbs

3 eggs, slightly beaten

1 cup Cheese, grated

2 Pimientos, chopped

½ Green Pepper, chopped fine

1 tablespoon Parsley Flakes

1 tablespoon Celery Flakes

½ teaspoon Onion Salt

⅛ teaspoon Cayenne

Blend all ingredients together, and spoon into 2 waxed paper lined, greased loaf pans. Set pans in a large one containing 1″ of hot water. Bake 1¼ hours at 300° F. Remove loaf pans from water, and set them on oven rack to bake another 10 to 15 minutes, or only until centers are just set (Macaroni "tightens" as it cools). Remove from oven, and let stand 15 minutes before unmolding onto platters. Garnish tops of loaves with Pimiento stars and Parsley. Serve with Mushroom Sauce.

This is delicious hot, and, surprisingly enough, it is almost as good cold.

OREGANO or WILD MARJORAM
(Herb)

❦❦❦

The Pizza Pie boom publicized this assertive, pleasantly bitter seasoning which is also popular in other Italian dishes. Prior to that food fad, the "Joy of the Mountain," as Oregano is called, was limited to use in the Southwest. The average home cook does not yet use Oregano to full advantage. What to do with it? Read on . . .

Chili Con Carne, Tamale Pie, Pork, Veal (Scallopini especially), *Meat Balls* or *Loaf, Game, Hamburger, Chicken, Duck, Lamb, Sausage; Stuffing* for any *Meat; Sweetbreads, Kidney* or *Beef Stew; Spaghetti Meat Sauces* (always);

Seafood Salads, Creamed Crab, Chowders, Fish Sauces;

Gumbos, Borscht, Minestrone, Bean or *Tomato Soup* (and other hearty Soups);

French Dressing;

Onions, Spinach, Squash, Leeks, Tomatoes (especially *Sauces*), *Eggplant, Peas, Cabbage, Broccoli, Potatoes; Vegeable Juices; Omelets, Scrambled Eggs.*

Greece, Chile, France, Mexico, and Italy supply us with the fresh or dried leaves of this perennial of the Mint family. (The fresh is limited to a few foreign shops.) Latin cooks are especially fond of fresh Wild Marjoram for seasoning *Lamb, Fowl, Stuffings,* and fresh *Mushroom Dishes.*

Oregano, which is an essential ingredient of Chili Powder, may be used much as Sweet Marjoram is, but Oregano requires more restraint. As with other herbs, Oregano should be added to long-cooking food only during the last hour of the cooking period. Dried Oregano is available whole or ground.

Oregano (the word is Spanish for Marjoram) is often used to give a rest to overworked Sage. In fact, Oregano is often called Mexican Sage, for Mexican cookery uses it enthusiastically.

Invite Oregano to your next cocktail party—*Tomato Juice Cocktails,* that is.

A Greek restaurant gave me a full appreciation of Oregano's worth, which I had previously doubted. During a meal I puzzled pleasantly over the delicious seasoning in *Braised Short Ribs of Beef.* Only after some minutes did I identify it as Oregano. (Oregano *must* be used lightly.)

My Favorite OREGANO Recipe

OREGANO SWISS STEAK

Slice of Round Steak, 1¼" thick
Salt, Pepper, Flour
¼ teaspoon Oregano

1 large Onion, minced
1 can Condensed Cream of Tomato Soup
½ can Water

2 tablespoons Bacon Drippings (or other Fat)

Season Steak well with Salt and Pepper, and then the Oregano. Beat Flour into Steak with edge of a small heavy plate, having Steak well coated with Flour. Sear Steak quickly in Bacon Fat in a very hot skillet. Reduce heat, and add other ingredients. Cover, and cook over very low heat 1½ hours, or until tender.

‰⧸‰

PAPRIKA
(Spice)

‰⧸‰

The day begins brightly if the *Breakfast Eggs* are sunny with a glow of "The Garnish Spice." And the day ends glowingly when the *Hashed Brown Potatoes* are Paprika-ed.

Orange-red Paprika—a sweet, gentle pepper which we import from Spain (although some grows in California)—can be dusted generously as a garnish on any *Creamed Meat, Fish, Cheese, Egg,* and *Chicken Dish.* Also, *Cabbage, Potatoes, Cauliflower*—Well, *all* color-short foods are improved by Paprika's dainty painting.

When garnishing a Crumb-topped casserole with Paprika, sprinkle the Spice on only after the food is almost baked, for too much dry heat darkens Paprika's lovely color,

Lettuce Cups for Salads are gay when their ruffled edges are dipped in Paprika, as is a *Lemon Slice* half-covered with the spice. (Young cook, use the Paprika-ed *Lemon Slice* to garnish *Fish* or *Cooked Greens*—never Iced Tea, for Paprika doesn't "go with" sweet things.)

Gourmets say Paprika's mild flavor blends especially well with those of *Shellfish, Fish, Sauces,* and *Salad Dressings.* This spice's flavor can range from sweet to pungently hot, depending on the variety of Paprika. One Hungarian Paprika is especially sweet and mild, although that country prefers its hot variety in its national dishes. (Hungary has a whole category of dishes known as "Paprikas.") Hungarian *Fish* and *Soups* especially use a generous quantity of this pepper. True Hungarian Paprika has disappeared behind the Iron Curtain. A Paprika similar to Hungary's hot one comes in limited quantity from Roumania and Yugoslavia, but it is available at only a few specialty shops. A bit of Cayenne added to the sweet Spanish Paprika makes a fair substitute for the genuine Hungarian variety.

Paprika is a toughy before being ground; the pods must be ground some eight times to make the spice fine enough for dusting, so we never see whole Paprikas.

Catsup and *Chili Sauce* use generous quantities of this red-colored pepper. *Hungarian Goulash* and *Chicken Paprika* both owe their rich color to it—a whole tablespoonful turns the trick. Vivid Paprika can transform unappetizingly gray *Meat Balls* into rosy successes. *Baked Potatoes,* like *Stuffed Celery,* look forlorn without Paprika.

Paprika should stand next to Salt and Pepper on the spice shelf, for these are cookery's most popular trio.

My Favorite PAPRIKA Recipe

OVEN-FRIED CHICKEN

Dip pieces of seasoned cut-up Fryer (floured or not, as you wish) in Melted Butter or Margarine, and sprinkle generously with Paprika. Place Chicken on a rimmed cookie pan, and bake uncovered at 450° until tender. Turn pieces of Chicken occasionally, and add more Paprika as needed to give the Chicken a bright color.

This easy method, which saves both shortening and time, turns out tasty Chicken. When cooking Chicken for a crowd, remember especially to try this method.

PARSLEY
(Herb)

Sautéed Parsley with *Broiled Mackerel* makes a toothsome two-some. Mediaeval cooks used sautéed-in-Butter Parsley as a *Soup Base*.

French-Fried Parsley has all the social graces; it's good company on any menu. (Just drop sprigs into deep hot fat for a few seconds.)

Coarsely-chopped Parsley can give both eye- and taste-appeal to *Tossed Salads*.

Curly Leaf Parsley makes a crowning complement for foods, just as it did for Roman heroes. (Shakespeare mentions Parsley's good looks.) A Parsley garnish is to be *eaten*, both for flavor and vitamins. And there's no rule against using this green both *in* and *on* a food.

Plain Leaf Parsley leads for seasoning foods. It goes into cooking foods just a moment or two before they're to come from the heat.

Parsley *Jelly* glamorizes *Meat*. Extract Parsley's flavor by steeping green sprigs or Parsley Flakes in scalding water, and then combine the essence with Apple Juice to make the jelly.)

This native of the Mediterranean area will grow abundantly in either a window box or a garden. (An old legend has it that an expectant mother can grow the best Parsley.)

Dry extra Parsley. Freeze extra Parsley. Dehydrated Parsley

Flakes, either of your own making or those from the spice counter, are insurance against finding you're a Parsley pauper.

Get your dime's worth when you buy fresh Parsley. Try for crisp green bunches. Then wash, clip, drain, and store in a covered jar. Your investment will pay bigger dividends if you take a moment each day to remove any fading or yellowing leaves.

Nibbling chlorophyll-ed Parsley after indulging in Garlic is a refreshing try.

Getting the idea from the Greeks, one clever hostess, when preparing for her husband's stag parties, places an egg-cup vase of decorative Parsley at each dinner plate to help keep fresh the soon-to-be-smoke-filled room.

Let's continue Parsleying our dishes both for garnish and goodness:

Vegetables; Meats, Seafoods, Poultry; Egg or *Cheese Dishes; Salads; Sauces; Soups; Everything*—except sweets.

Even *Stuffings* need Parsley, for three tablespoons of freshly minced Parsley can give wings to Sage's heavy flavor in Sage Dressing. And *Pizza Pie* becomes a prideful pie when seasoned with a teaspoon each of Parsley, Rosemary, Marjoram, and Thyme. (Omit the usual Oregano.)

My Favorite PARSLEY Recipe

CORN MUFFINS
(*1 dozen*)

½ cup Yellow Corn Meal
½ cup Boiling Water
2 tablespoons Butter or Margarine
½ cup sifted all-purpose Flour
½ cup Milk

2 tablespoons freshly minced Parsley (or 1 of Flakes)
½ teaspoon Onion Salt
1 tablespoon Sugar
2 teaspoons Baking Powder
1 Egg, beaten very light

Stir the Boiling Water into the Corn Meal, and add the Shortening, beating well. Cover, and let stand 2 hours. Sift the dry ingredients together, and add them to the first mixture. Then add the Parsley, Milk, and the Egg, mixing well. Pour the thin batter into preheated, well greased muffin tins, and bake 20-25 minutes at 425° F.

❧§❧

BLACK or WHITE PEPPER
(Spice)

❧§❧

Pepper is the only spice that rates a shaker of its own at the table at every meal. (Salt is a chemical.)

This richest treasure of the spice chest is esteemed today just as much as it was in the Middle Ages when rents were often required to be paid in Peppercorns. America uses 55% Pepper as compared to 45% for all other spices!

The price of this spice has been high since World War II, for the supply has dropped 71% in the past decade, due to Japanese devastation of the Pepper vines in Indonesia and also postwar political difficulties in the islands.

To keep your Pepper bill down, store this spice as far from heat as possible; heat causes its flavor to weaken quickly. And nothing's so disappointing as Black Pepper that doesn't taste like Black Pepper.

Why is White Pepper a minor mystery to many people? White and Black Pepper have similar flavors, but White's is somewhat less biting. White is preferred for seasoning *creamed* and other dishes in which a diner might look askance at black specks, and also in dishes which call for a more gentle bite than Black Pepper would give. Many cooks prefer White Pepper in *Poultry*.

Fresh Peppercorns, which look like clusters of red currants, are picked before fully ripe, then cleaned and dried, during which process they turn dark. That's the way Black Pepper is made. White Pepper is made from fully-ripened berries from which the outer coat has been removed.

Black Pepper ranges in color from yellow-white to dark brown or black. White ranges from light gray to tan.

Pepper is an especially healthful spice; it helps in converting our food into energy. This spice is recommended for seasoning the food of salt-free dieters. Pepper aids digestion and helps promote a good appetite.

Although Pepper was used in Sausage during the Crusades, it was only in 1947 that this spice was proved to have a preservative effect upon *Sausage Meats*.

Pepper could be found only on the tables of the wealthy in ancient times. In fact, ransoms were sometimes required to be paid in it. A fabulous three thousand pounds of Pepper was part of the ransom of Rome to Alaric, the Visigoth, when he lay siege to Rome in 408 A.D. (Even these barbarians knew spices would make their food more interesting.) When all of Magellan's ships but the Victoria foundered, the Pepper in the surviving ship more than paid for the financial loss of the other four vessels.

Black Pepper (and other spices) probably hastened America's discovery, for Columbus won financial backers by convincing them he might find spices on his voyage. Much later, America's Merchant Marine was founded by brave Yankee skippers who brought millions of dollars' worth of Black Pepper to Salem from 1795 to 1846, making Salem the world center of the Pepper trade at that time. Pirates finally put an end to Colonial America's spice trade which first began with Captain Jonathan Carnes' voyage of 1795 that yielded a seven hundred percent profit! New York is the spice trading capital of the world today.

The twenty-foot Pepper vine, which is trained to climb poles or other supports much as grape vines are, is native to the East Indies. India and Indonesia supply most of our Black Pepper.

Pepper, the best liked of all spices, is standard seasoning for *Meats, Poultry, Fish, Egg* and *Cheese Dishes,* and *Vegetables.*

(Also see PEPPERCORN.)

❦❦❦

RED PEPPER

❦❦❦

There are many types of Red Peppers available whole, crushed, or ground, and only experience can tell any cook the kind best suited to her own taste.

In general, Red Pepper in any of its forms may be used in *Pickles, Relishes, Hot Sauces, Gravies, Stews, Mixed Greens, Meats, Navy Beans,* etc.

(Also see CAYENNE.)

My Favorite RED PEPPER Recipe

PEPPER SAUCE

Fill a small bottle with Whole or Crushed Red Peppers, and cover with Cider Vinegar. Let ripen three weeks before using.

This simple sauce adds much zest to *Cabbage, Cooked Greens, White Beans, Sauces,* and *Seafoods.*

PEPPERCORNS
(Spice)

Whole Peppercorns mean hotter, more aromatic, and pungent Pepper than the ready-ground can give you.

At the best tables, the wrinkled little Peppercorns (600 weigh an ounce!) are ground right onto food. A tiny artistic mill, which adds beauty to the table, does the grinding. Such mills are available from gift and novelty shops and spice packers.

Open-Faced Tomato Sandwiches enter the party chatter only when they carry the bite of freshly-grated Peppercorns.

Whole Peppercorns are highly preferred for seasoning *Stews, Pot Roasts,* and *Pickles.* Meat packers know Peppercorns' value in *Pressed Spiced Meats.*

Landlords of the Middle Ages preferred (and often demanded) their rents in precious Peppercorns. In the Eleventh Century some towns even kept their accounts in terms of Peppercorns' worth. Nearer home, Lyndhurst, New Jersey, recently paid 150 years' back rent on a schoolhouse in Peppercorns, as specified in the original grant.

Though unimpressive in appearance, the little Peppercorn can give the zenith of zest to our foods.

(Also see BLACK AND WHITE PEPPER.)

My Favorite PEPPERCORN Recipe

SPICED SHRIMP

10 Peppercorns	1 Green Pepper, chopped
3 Bay (Laurel) Leaves	(seed and all)
1 teaspoon Whole Cloves	2 tablespoons Salt
2 Lemons, sliced thin	5 Cloves of Garlic
¼ teaspoon Cayenne	1 teaspoon Celery Seed

1 cup Vinegar

Boil the above ingredients in 1½ gallons Water 15 minutes. Then drop 3 pounds fresh Shrimp into the boiling mixture. (If Frozen Shrimp are used they should be first thawed and then washed.) Boil covered 8 or 9 minutes, or until Shrimp are just tender. Test for doneness by breaking a Shrimp; it should still be slightly crisp when done. Drain and serve hot immediately, with bowls of Cocktail Sauce and Drawn Butter, each man to shell his own Shrimp. Or the Shrimp may be cooled in their cooking water and then be shelled, chilled, and used for Cocktails or Salads.

≈§§≈

PICKLING SPICE
(Combination)

≈§§≈

Fourteen countries are represented in a box of Whole Pickle Spice, a "must-have" for every spice shelf. Some sixteen different spices are contained in this beautiful balance of flavors which is certainly not to be limited to *Pickles*. (Since packing spices in jars with Pickles darkens them, in preparing Cooked Pickles, tie spices in a loose cheesecloth bag and drop it into the simmering Pickles. Remove and discard spice bag before packing Pickles.)

This mixture of whole spices is handy for seasoning *Fish Stews, Soups, Barbecue Sauce, Sauerkraut, Stewed Tomatoes, Boiled Beets* (especially *Harvard Beets*), *Buttered Cabbage, Game,* and *Braised* or *Stewed Meats.*

And a bit of Pickling Spice is a benediction to the *Butter Sauce* for any *Hot Vegetable.*

In meat cookery, this combination is especially useful in preparing *Marinades* for *Game, Beef, Hasenpfeffer, Sauerbraten,* and *Shellfish.*

Pickling Spice are ideal for preparing *Spice Shrimp*: Tie a handful of the spices in cheesecloth, and drop the bag into boiling water. Cover, and let simmer 15 minutes. Add Salt and Shrimp. Boil Shrimp 8 or 9 minutes or until just tender. Serve hot with Drawn Butter or Cocktail Sauce. Or let cool in their cooking water, and then shell, chill, and use the Shrimp for Salads and Cocktails. Shrimp for any purpose are best when cooked with spices.

When the last *Pickled Peach* or *Sweet Pickle* is used from a jar, use the tart-sweet sirup lightly for seasoning *Mayonnaise,* and generously for basting *Baking Ham*.

My Favorite PICKLING SPICE *Recipe*

CRISP SWEET PICKLES

Soak 7 pounds sliced Cucumbers 24 hours in 1 gallon Water to which ½ cup Lime has been added. Then wash Pickles, and soak in clear Water another 12 hours. Then drain, and soak for 12 hours in 3 quarts Cider Vinegar in which 5 pounds Sugar has been dissolved by stirring.

Set the Pickles on the heat, add 4 tablespoons Pickling Spice (tied in a cheesecloth bag) and 3 tablespoons Salt and 1 tablespoon Whole Fennel Seed. Cook until Vinegar becomes sirupy, about 30 minutes. Seal Pickles in jars.

These Pickles have an excellent flavor and a good color.

❧

PIE AND PUDDING SPICE
(Blend)

❧

This mouth-watering potpourri of Cinnamon, Cloves, Ginger, etc., is used in the *Holiday Pies—Pumpkin,* of course. But don't overlook this spice for flavoring *Pecan, Sweet Potato,* and *Squash Pies; Bread Pudding,* and *Black Bean Soup!*

Also let this blend add festive flavor to *Whipped Cream* for topping any dessert.

Sweet Rolls, Molasses Cookies, Rice Pudding, Sweet Potatoes, and *Fruit Salad Dressing* are some of the other many foods that Pie and Pudding Spice can improve.

Even the best home cook would find it difficult to match this flavor balance. It is safe to take at face value every superlative an advertiser attaches to this winning blend.

My Favorite PIE AND PUDDING SPICE Recipe

SPICY PECAN PIE

Cream 3 tablespoons Butter, and gradually add 1 cup Sugar and ⅓ teaspoon Salt. Add 3 Eggs that have been beaten very light, mixing thoroughly. Then stir in 1 cup Dark Corn Sirup, 1 teaspoon Pie and Pudding Spice, and 1 teaspoon Vanilla. Add 1¼ cups Pecan Halves.

Pour mixture into an unbaked Pie Shell that has been brushed with Melted Butter or Margarine and then chilled thoroughly. Bake at 325° F. 45 minutes, or until center of the pie is set.

PIMIENTOS

Without Pimiento the world of Cheeses would be less colorful. Perhaps everyone's first acquaintance with this pepper is in *Pimiento Cheese*.

The fleshy, orange-red sweet Spanish Paprika is canned, whole chopped, in oil.

Pimiento is a ubiquitous, but always welcome garnish. It appears as full-blown tulips, shooting stars, pinked strips, and in many other forms, depending on the artistry of the hand that creates the garnish.

Pimiento's bland but piquant flavor and flaming color make this gentle pepper adaptable as an ingredient of or a garnish for any *Creamed Vegetable, Meat,* or *Seafood Dish*.

Have you discovered what a beauty it is chopped up in the *Butter Sauce* for *Steamed Cauliflower*? And Pimiento is something else to do for that colorless *Rice Ring*.

My Favorite PIMIENTO Recipe

MACARONI SALAD

2 cups cooked Macaroni

1 small can or jar of Chopped Pimientos, drained

½ cup diced, unpared Cucumber

1 cup finely chopped Celery

½ Green Pepper, chopped

¾ cup Mayonnaise

½ teaspoon Onion Salt

⅛ teaspoon Black Pepper

Combine all ingredients, and chill. Serve in Lettuce Cups. Garnish with Cucumber Slices and a Pimiento Strip.

PINE CONES

⤜⧏⧎⤛

Romanian cookery uses Pine Cones, whole or ground, to season *Smoked Pork, Sauces* for *Game,* and *Marinades* for *Fish* and *Meats.* (The idea is not too far removed from our use of Juniper Berries.)

POPPY SEED
(Seed)

Buttered Cauliflower peppered with Poppy Seed is an easy to achieve masterpiece. A teaspoon of the walnut-flavored Seed can be added to the *Butter Sauce* for any *Hot Vegetable.* They *should* be added to supper's *Scrambled Eggs.*

And these are worthy Seed sprinkled lightly in *French Onion Soup.*

Baked in or on *Breads,* the crunchy, kidney-shaped (they look round to the eye) Seed have a nutty flavor.

Nine hundred thousand Poppy Seed make a pound. One hundred twenty-five thousand of them added to the *Dark Fruit Cake* batter will give the Cake a more interesting texture and a rich nutty flavor. (Just measure about half a cup for the Cake.)

The Dutch cultivate the Poppy that produces the best of the tiny fragrant blue seeds. A white variety, which is often dyed to look like the quality blue ones, comes from Poland, Turkey, Hungary, and Czechoslovakia.

A delicious *Sweet Roll Filling* is made by mixing Jam and Poppy Seed. The Seed are often used in *Cake Fillings,* especially those made of a *Custard* base; also in *Biscuits, Cheese Dishes, Meat* or *Cream Cheese Spreads, Candies, Cookies, Buttered Noodles, Sweet Potatoes, and Fruit* or *Vegetable Salads.*

Youngsters like a *Bread Spread* made of Honey and Poppy Seed. Everyone will like your next *Cookie Crumb Pie Shell* more than usual if you add 3 tablespoons Poppy Seed to the crumbs.

My Favorite POPPY SEED Recipe

HONEY-GLAZED CARROTS

3 tablespoons Honey
2 tablespoons Butter or Margarine

¼ teaspoon grated Orange Rind
1 tablespoon Poppy Seed
⅛ teaspoon Salt

Combine the above ingredients in a skillet, and bring to a boil. Add 10 or 12 tiny Carrots, so young they need not be scraped, that have been boiled in salted water until just tender. Simmer the Carrots in the glaze 10 to 12 minutes, turning the Carrots frequently.

≈§≈

PORK: SALT PORK, FAT BACK, SOWSBELLY, STEAKED MEAT, STREAK O'LEAN, HOG JOWL, WHITE SIDE PORK

≈§≈

The earthy colloquial names for Pork will be denied by many Southerners. Although the terms are not often used publicly the realistic terms do exist and give much color to the market list. But this, our favorite seasoning, shouldn't be belittled, for it adds a meaty richness to what otherwise might be watery vegetables.

Salt Pork, which is any fat cut of Pork preserved in Salt, is a marvelous seasoning for *Turnips, Dried Peas* and *Beans, Green Beans, Cooked Greens, Cabbage,* and *Squash.* Some form of Pork, usually Bacon or Salt Pork, is used to enrich *Gumbos,* and *Clam* and *Fish Chowders.* But I never expected to find Pork in *Boiled Potatoes!* Surprisingly satisfying, but my own hand can't combine the two.

An overly enthusiastic copywriter must have started the misnomer *Pork and Beans* for those popular canned-in-Tomato-Sauce Beans. *One* tiny cube of cooked-to-death Pork to a can! "Beans and Pork" would not even be appropriate. Misnamed or not, America loves them.

Here's a trick-and-treat: After cooking some Vegetable with Pork, remove the tender block of white meat, rinse under running hot water, cool, and then refrigerate the meat. At midnight snack time, slice the waxy tidbit thinly, and eat it on Crackers with Herb Mustard, or just Salt and Pepper. Next time you won't wait for the clock to strike twelve.

184

Tennessee's famous *Spiced Round of Beef,* a Christmas Meat, depends on Lardoons, spiced strips of White Pork, for its succulence. (See LARDOONS.)

Hog Jowl is used so promptly it is not often necessary to preserve it by salting. Eating *Hog Jowl and Black-Eyed Peas,* called *Hoppinjohn,* on New Year's Day will bring you good luck throughout the New Year. At least, no food can be more satisfying than this homely dish is after all the rich foods of the Holiday Season.

Don't underestimate Pork as a seasoning. Even a tired-looking Ham Bone can greatly enliven *Pea* or *Bean Soup.* Just a bit of Pork can give a bang to many different dishes.

My Favorite PORK Recipe

RICH GREEN BEANS

Green Beans in Butter Sauce are impalatable to exiled Southerners who are used to Beans cooked with Streaked Meat. For the uninitiated, here's the old-time way of preparing them. (The same tactics are used to enrich other vegetables with Pork.)

Place ¼ pound Salt Pork or Streaked Meat in a small quantity of water; cover, place over high heat. When it comes to a boil, reduce heat, and let simmer until the meat is almost tender. String, break, and wash a couple pounds of Pole Beans, and drop them into the steaming pot. Add a teaspoon of Sugar (not enough to taste), 1¼ teaspoons Salt, and Cayenne if desired. Cover Beans, and bring to a quick boil. Let bubble merrily about 10 minutes, or until Beans are half-tender. Then reduce heat, and continue cooking until all the liquid has disappeared, stirring occasionally. Serve with Corn Bread, Bermuda Onion, and Tomatoes.

Green beans cooked in this manner are a good meat substitute. (Any leftover beans will be even tastier the second day.)

POULTRY SEASONING
(Blend)

The hand of a genius must toss together this mixture of Sage, Thyme, Marjoram, Savory, Rosemary, etc., which is used to season the obvious. This seasoning is also a good picker-upper for *Hamburgers, Croquettes, Dumplings, Stuffings, Meat Loaf, Fish, Pork, Meat Balls, Biscuits, Corn Bread*, and *French-Fried Onions*. (For the Onions, add ⅛ teaspoon Poultry Seasoning to the batter.)

And this savory serenade is more than harmonious in *Cream Gravy* to go with *Fried Chicken*—or in *Waffles* to be topped with *Creamed Chicken*.

My Favorite POULTRY SEASONING Recipe

SPOON BREAD POULTRY DRESSING
(Casserole)

1 cup Yellow Corn Meal	½ teaspoon Poultry Seasoning
3 cups cold Chicken Broth	½ cup Celery, chopped very fine
3 tablespoons Chicken Fat or Butter or Margarine	2 pimientos, chopped fine
3 teaspoons Baking Powder	2 tablespoons freshly minced Parsley (or 1 of Flakes)
1 teaspoon Onion Flakes	⅛ teaspoon Black Pepper
2 hard-boiled Eggs, grated	Salt to taste
2 Eggs, well beaten	

186

Stir Meal into Cold Broth. Bring slowly to a boil, stirring constantly. Then reduce heat, and cook until thickened, stirring constantly. Add Chicken Fat. Remove from heat, and add other ingredients. Pour into a greased casserole. Bake 40 minutes at 350° F. Serve with Baked Chicken and Giblet Gravy.

❧§§❧

PUMPKIN PIE SPICE
(Blend)

❧§§❧

Pumpkin Pie is another food that can be most uninteresting if not flavored wisely. Pumpkin Pie Spice holds that wisdom.

This merry mixture is also pleasant in *Applesauce, Bread* or *Rice Pudding*—and as a quick accurate answer to the question, "How to get that 'sameness' out of today's *Cake?*" Add Pumpkin Pie Spice to the *Frosting!*

My *Favorite* PUMPKIN PIE SPICE Recipe

SPEEDY SPICE CAKE

Sift together 2 cups sifted all-purpose Flour, 1 tablespoon double-acting Baking Powder, 2 teaspoons Pumpkin Pie Spice, 1 teaspoon Salt, and ¾ cup granulated Sugar. Add ½ cup Vegetable Shortening, ½ cup Brown Sugar (well packed), and ¾ cup Milk. Beat well.

Add ¼ cup more Milk, 2 Eggs, 1 teaspoon Vanilla, and beat thoroughly.

Bake in 2 well-greased, floured 8″ cake pans at 350° F. 40 minutes. Cool, and frost with Browned Butter Icing (See BUTTER for recipe).

This cake's good flavor is an achievement of today's short-cut cookery methods and the spice blenders.

PURSLANE
(Herb)

Robert Herrick, the English poet, wrote of Purslane, one of the ancient herbs. The cook writes in her notes:

"Use Purslane's tender leaves in *Tossed Salads*. Also in *Vegetable Soups,* as the French do."

These succulent leaves may also be cooked as *Greens,* too, to be served with a Lemony Sauce.

⌘

ROASTMEAT SEASONING
(Blend)

⌘

Escoffier himself might have created this blend of Thyme, Powdered Onion, Salt, Garlic, Red Pepper, and other spices.

You can use it confidently, for it gives a princely flavor to *Meat*—just any Meat at all.

It's a *before cooking* seasoning, so rub the blend on all sides of Meat before cooking, whether you're braising, broiling, boiling, frying, stewing, or roasting.

And don't let the name slow you down, for this blend is also delicious in *Soups, Stews, Omelets, Creamed Cheese* or *Egg Dishes*—and in *Vegetables*. Your family will linger over every bite of every dish you make taste-tempting with this gourmet gremlin, a good one.

My Favorite ROASTMEAT SEASONING Recipe

CORN PUDDING

Soak 4 tablespoons Quick-Cooking Minute Tapioca in 2 cups Cold Milk in top of a double boiler 5 minutes. Cook in double boiler 15 minutes, stirring occasionally. Pour a small amount of mixture over 2 well-beaten Eggs, stirring well. Add Eggs to hot mixture, and mix thoroughly. Add:

1 tablespoon Parsley Flakes
1 teaspoon Onion Flakes
1 teaspoon Roastmeat Seasoning

1 No. 2 can Yellow Corn (2½ cups)
2 Pimientos, finely chopped
1 tablespoon Olive Oil

Pour mixture into a greased casserole, and set it in a pan of hot water in a 325° F. oven. Bake 1¼ hours, or until center is just set. This Corn Pudding holds up better than the Custard type.

ROSE GERANIUM

Before picking a few Rose Geranium Leaves to lay in the bottom of the *Pound Cake* pan, Grandmother would crush one fragrant leaf between her fingers and then stand lost in her pleasure of its roselike perfume.

Your guests also may be lost in their pleasure of your Geranium-flavored *Jellies, Baked Pears, Fruit Compotes, Ice Cream Sauce, Fruit Punch, Cake Frostings,* and *Rice* and other *Custard Puddings.* The idea is to place a Fresh Geranium leaf or two in the bottom of the baking dish, freezing tray, fruit cup, etc.

Rose Geranium's dried petals are used in herb *Teas* (also in potpourris), and the oil from the foliage is prized in hand lotions, soaps, and perfumes.

Two or three fresh sprays of this easy-to-grow plant, plus a light dash of red food coloring, can turn your next batch of *Apple Jelly* into *Rose Geranium Jelly.*

ROSE PETALS

The Queen of Flowers makes a queenly *Vinegar*. Steep the dried petals of any fragrant roses in Wine Vinegar until your tasting spoon can catch the elusive flavor of the petals. This epicurean Vinegar can give an exquisite touch to *Fruit Salad Dressings*.

Fresh Rose Petals, either as a garnish or an ingredient, can give a delicate aroma and flavor to *Fruit Cups* or *Salads, Apple Jelly, Honey, Melon Balls,* and other light-flavored foods. (A stronger Rose flavor is obtained by crushing a couple of petals and blending them into food.) A *Rose Pudding,* which may have been a Custard, was one of Nero's special treats.

Wild Rose Jelly is an unforgettable taste experience. Five 6-ounce glasses are made thus:

Scald 2¼ cups Apple Juice, and pour it over 1 quart Wild Rose Petals. Boil 15 minutes. Strain through a jelly bag. (There should be 2 cups now.) Add 3½ cups Sugar to the hot Juice, and mix well, adding a drop or two of Red Food Coloring to give a delicate color. Bring to a rolling boil, stirring constantly. Then mix in quickly ½ bottle Liquid Fruit Pectin. Boil hard 1 minute, stirring all the while. Remove from heat, skim, and pour quickly into glasses. Cover with paraffin at once. (An even more epicurean Jelly can be made by replacing the Apple Juice with 2 cups Water and ¼ cup *fresh* Strawberry Juice.)

Delicate-flavored Rose Water has moved from the spice shelf to the cosmetic shelf, but this Water is still used occasionally to flavor *Pound Cakes*.

Rose Petals have been prized as a culinary delicacy for centuries. India has long enjoyed them candied, as also does England. An occasional specialty house features *Rose Conserves*. Wines and liqueurs were first made of Rose Petals centuries ago. *Glacé Roses* are a party delicacy, prepared by thoughtful hostesses who know the beautiful tidbits make for delightful conversation and nibbling. Hostesses also float Fresh Rose Petals in *Punch Cups*.

The Queen of Flowers, which grows practically all over the world, can knight any *Fruit Dish* at all, for there is an especial affinity between the two flavors. Our Grandmothers had this in mind when they dropped a few fresh petals in the bottom of each *Jelly* glass.

ଏବ୍ରି

ROSEMARY
(Herb)

ଏବ୍ରି

If you don't yet know Rosemary an easy introduction can be arranged. Just drop a bit of Rosemary into the cooking water for any *Green Vegetable*.

Rosemary's pungent, fresh or dried leaves, which look like miniature curved pine needles, can give exciting goodness and garnish to:

Fruit Cups, Fruit Salads; Jams, Sauces, Wines, Vinegars; Fish, Creamed Crab;

Roast Beef, Meat Stews, Poultry, Stuffings, Rabbit, Lamb, Pork, Veal, Meat Salads;

Chicken, Pea, or Turtle Soup; Biscuits, Corn Bread;

Potatoes, Eggplant, Green Beans, Spinach, Swiss Chard, Turnips, Cauliflower.

"The Meat Herb" is especially excellent on *Lamb* (which can get along very well without Garlic occasionally). Rosemary, whose flavor is somewhat like a blend of Sage and Thyme, combines well with Parsley, Garlic, Chives, or Thyme.

"There's Rosemary, that's for remembrance," said Ophelia. In England, this herb still plays a remembrance role, for it is often placed on the graves of English heroes. The Romans, who used Rosemary to decorate their banquet halls and churches, introduced the plant to England where brides began tucking this symbol of fidelity into their bouquets.

Most of our Rosemary, which is available whole or ground, comes from France, Spain, Yugoslavia, and Portugal. In Europe pillows are often stuffed with Rosemary and Pine Needles.

Italian cooks are devoted to Rosemary, which is said to grow only in the gardens of the righteous. Another of the many legends about this evergreen herb declares that sleeping with a sprig of it under our pillows will keep bad dreams away. We *know* Rosemary can keep monotony from our menus.

My Favorite ROSEMARY Recipe

MEAT LOAF

2 pounds Ground Beef (preferably Round Steak)	1 small jar chopped Pimientos
½ pound Ground Pork	1 cup soft Bread Crumbs
½ pound Ground Veal	2 teaspoons Onion Flakes
1 tablespoon Flavor Salt	2 teaspoons Parsley Flakes
3 Eggs	1 can Condensed Cream of
½ teaspoon Rosemary	Tomato Soup, diluted with ½ can Water

Combine ingredients, and mix well. Shape into loaf, and bake 1 hour at 350° F.

❧❅❧

RUE
(Herb)

❧❅❧

Rue's bitter, almost moldy flavor is intriguing in *Green Salads*. In the garden Rue's odor is unpleasant, but herb growers love the plant's shining beauty.

Fresh or dried, the bluish-green leaves can restore interest in an ordinary *Meat Stew* or a plain *Cottage Cheese Salad*.

Rue's unusually pungent flavor is also oddly pleasing in:

Braised Beef, Creamed Chicken, Lamb Stew; Fish, Tuna Fish Salad;

Egg or *Cheese Dishes; Cheese Spreads* for dark-bread hors-d'oeuvres;

Cranberry Juice, Vegetable Juices; Aromatic Vinegars;

Creamed Potatoes, Vegetable Salads, Mushroom Dishes.

A *Green Salad* tossed by an Italian cook often carries a few Rue leaves.

This herb was thought by the Greeks and the Romans to protect them from diseases. Sprigs of Rue were once used to sprinkle holy water over a repentant sinner's head; over the ages the herb became symbolic of repentance.

SAFFLOWER
(Herb)

❧❦❧

This herb, which is frequently called "False Saffron," has often been substituted for expensive Saffron for coloring *Cakes* and *Confections*.

Safflower is a thistlelike plant which has orange-yellow flowers from which a dyestuff is made. Safflower can color food quite satisfactorily, but its flavor is disappointing.

SAFFRON
(Spice)

Saffron is the world's most expensive spice. Nuremberg dealers of the 1400's who were caught adulterating it were burned at the stake.

Today Spanish Saffron sells for about fifty dollars a pound. No wonder. Seventy-five thousand flowers must be gathered and three stigma removed from each—all by hand—two hundred twenty-five thousand in all, to make a pound of Saffron. Expensive, yes, but a little Saffron, which can give Midas's golden touch to food, goes a long way. A few Saffron stigma may be purchased for thirty cents at some supermarkets.

In cookery, Saffron, which is imported from the Mediterranean area, is often added to the other ingredients in tea form; the infusion imparts an intriguing Oriental flavor that is pleasantly bitter and also a rich yellow color. Saffron's golden hue was ancient Greece's royal color; this spice was used to dye the royal robes.

Saffron is used in *Plain* and *Sweet Breads, Cakes, Chicken Dishes* (this use has been popular since mediaeval times), *Fish Sauces, Bouillabaisse, Curried Dishes,* and *Rice*. In using Saffron in Rice, the spice should be added to the boiling water a few minutes before the Rice is.

The Cornish have a nostalgic love for Saffron. Their "Fuggins" are Saffron-flavored Sweet Buns. Legend relates that this spice was introduced into Cornwall by survivors of the Spanish Armada.

King Solomon's gardens of about 1,000 B.C. were graced with the perennial, purple, crocuslike flowers from which Saffron comes. (The Bible records that this ruler gained much wealth from spice traffic.) Ancient Romans perfumed their baths with Saffron.

Arabian Nights mentions Saffron as an aphrodisiac. The Arabs once believed that keeping Saffron in their houses warded off the appearance of a certain dreaded lizard. Also, the same people thought Saffron dispelled melancholy.

Court ladies of Henry VIII's reign tinted their hair with Saffron until that monarch forbade it; he feared a Saffron shortage that might reach his own table.

"Crocodile tears," a vague legend relates, were first shed by the crocodile in his joy over Saffron's perfume.. (Makes him seem a better fellow than does the legend of his mock tears over his victims.)

Today Saffron's perfume and flavor are especially famous in two Spanish dishes: *Arroz con Pollo* (Chicken and Rice), which is popular in Florida where it is served with crunchy, crusty Cuban Bread; and *Bacalao Vizcaino* (Cod Fish à la Biscay).

My Favorite SAFFRON Recipe

SAFFRON SAUCE FOR CHICKEN-CORN BREAD SANDWICHES

Sauté 4 minced Onions in ½ pound Butter or Margarine until lightly browned. Remove and discard Onions. Add to the Onion-seasoned Butter or Margarine:

> 4 cups Chicken Stock from Hen that has been simmered
> until tender in Water to cover, with 2 Celery Stalks,
> 1 sliced Carrot, ¼ teaspoon Saffron, 2 teaspoons Salt
> 1 pint light Cream

1 tablespoon Worcestershire Sauce
⅛ teaspoon each Cayenne and Curry Powder and Allspice
2 tablespoons Sherry
1 teaspoon Sugar

Heat the sauce thoroughly, and then bind it with 3 tablespoons Flour that have been rubbed into 3 tablespoons Chicken Fat. (The sauce should be thin.) Serve over sliced Chicken on squares of Corn Bread.

SAGE
(Herb)

Sage is synonomous with *Stuffing*.

Although often misused, Sage is still one of America's most popular food seasonings. This familiar perennial Mint, which has a powerfully fragrant and pleasantly bitter flavor, is used—preferably with rigid restraint—to season:

Dried Beef, Duck, Goose, Chicken, Turkey, Sausage, Veal, Stews, Hamburgers, Pork Chops, Meat Stuffings of all kinds;
Baked Fish, Salt Cod, Chowders;
Cream Gravies, Canned Soups, Salad Dressings;
Stewed Tomatoes, Eggplant, Green Beans, Onions, Cabbage, Mashed Potatoes, Turnips, Brussels Sprouts;
Cheese Casseroles, Cottage Cheese, Creamed Eggs.

Crushed fresh Sage Leaves give pleasing personality to *Cottage Cheese Salads*. Sage Cheeses have been marketed for centuries. Your own version can be made by blending a bit of Sage into grated *Cheese* which has been creamed with a little Mayonnaise. For Sandwiches, of course. The Dutch enjoy a Sage-flavored *Hot Milk Drink*.

Many cooks declare Sage too strong for seasoning Chicken and Turkey and urge substituting equal parts of Thyme, Marjoram, and Rosemary. In fact, Americans seem to be the only people who are enthusiastic over Sage in Poultry.

A sage suggestion: When using Sage it's a good idea to use a double quantity of Parsley, for Parsley seems to civilize Sage's barbaric flavor. Even cooks of the Middle Ages paired these two.

Although many herbs are equally tasty fresh or dried, Sage is better fresh (as are also Chervil and Mint). In fact, the flavor of Green Sage is quite different from that of Dried.

Sage will grow easily in the garden, either from seed or cuttings. *Sage Tea,* made from her own herbs, was a favorite of my grandmother—and perhaps also of yours. At the spice counter, Sage is available in three forms: whole leaf, crushed, or powdered.

A variety of wild Sage is imported in great quantity from Yugoslavia. Still more comes from Spain, Italy, and Greece. (Our own wild sagebrush has a turpentine flavor.)

Savory or Oregano make a good substitute for overworked Sage, which, by the way, is the most limited in use of all herbs, simply because we tire of the strong flavor. But Sage's flavor will serve us well when not abused.

"How can a man die in whose garden Sage is growing?" asks an old wise saying of Roman times. Too-frequent or too-heavy use of Sage can cause one's taste for it to die.

My Favorite SAGE Recipe

PORK CHOP DINNER

Mrs. Lora French Logan of Alton, Illinois, passed this dinner-in-one-skillet recipe on to me.

Melt 1 tablespoon Shortening in heavy skillet that has a tight-fitting lid. Dip 6 thin center-cut Pork Chops in Sage-seasoned Flour (⅛ to ¼ teaspoon Sage to a cup of Flour), and brown in the hot Fat.

Slice 4 Potatoes and 4 Onions. Remove 3 of the Chops from skillet, and place a layer of Potatoes and Onions on the 3 Chops remaining in skillet. Season with Salt and Pepper. Add the other Chops and the remaining Potatoes and Onions. Pour ½ cup hot water over all. Cover, and cook 30 minutes. Then add 4 Tomatoes and 1 Green Pepper which have been sliced and a little additional Salt and Pepper. Cook 15 minutes longer.

SALT

(Chemical)

This seasoning is indispensable to man's food and health. No one has ever bothered to think up a catchy name for it. No one needs to, for we will always buy Salt.

We don't need recipes to tell us how to use Salt; our palates tell us. With experience, we can figure out how much Salt to put in any kind of dish. However, since both too little Salt and certainly too much can spoil food, definite proportions will get the inexperienced cook off to a satisfactorily-salted start:

Hot Cereals: Use 1 teaspoon Salt to 2 cups liquid for cooking.

Doughs: Use 1 teaspoon Salt to 4 cups Four. (When multiplying baking recipes, the Salt may need reducing somewhat.)

Meats: Use 1 teaspoon Salt to 1 pound Meat.

Sauces and *Soups*: Use 1 teaspoon Salt to 1 quart Soup or Sauce. (For too-salty Soup, add sliced Potatoes to absorb some of the Salt. Discard Potatoes before serving Soup.)

Vegetables: Use ½ teaspoon Salt to 1 pound Vegetables requiring 1 quart cooking water. (Green Beans especially must have adequate Salt cooked into them, for it is difficult to salt them properly after they are cooked.)

A fairy pinch of Salt makes good *Coffee* better. *Fruit Punches,* too.

Herb-flavored Salts, which contain ground dried herbs, impart a more delicate flavor to foods than the herbs alone would give.

When using flavored Salts, be sure to reduce the plain Salt. Incidentally, Flavor Salt is an excellent all-purpose seasoning for *Vegetables, Meat Dishes, Sauces, Soups,* and *Salads.*

The seasoning rule "too little rather than too much" must have referred originally to Salt, for there is little to be done to redeem most too-Salty foods.

My Favorite FLAVOR SALT Recipe

VEGETABLE SAUCE

Add the following to 1 cup melted Sweet Butter:

1 teaspoon Flavor Salt	½ teaspoon Paprika
1 tablespoon Parsley Flakes	1 tablespoon Lemon Juice

This quick Sauce is especially tasty on *Hot Green Vegetables* and *Potatoes.*

SASSAFRAS

The ground leaves of this American tree of the laurel family is the essential ingredient of Filé Powder which is a popular seasoning in Creole cookery, especially for *Gumbos*. (See GUMBO FILÉ.) The Creoles learned this seasoning trick from the Choctaw Indians. Oil of Sassafras, which is distilled from the tree's bark and roots, is used for flavoring *Soft Drinks* and *Candies*.

Tea is made of Sassafras Roots. (Some gift houses featured Smoked Sassafras Root.) The tea is an oldtime but still popular home remedy for purifying the blood. Many enthusiasts drink it for its fine flavor and lovely tawny color; the tea can be a tasty experience if not boiled too long, which makes it bitter. I brew it occasionally just to enjoy its aroma.

Almost every little independent grocer in the country carries a supply of the prized red roots; they are usually tied in neat miniature bundles. I've also seen the roots in supermarkets of national fame. The large split roots are to be avoided; they are lacking in flavor.

If you set out to dig your own Sassafras roots you'll soon need to rest. Then notice that this tree has leaves of three different shapes.

❧❦❧

SAUSAGE SEASONING
(Blend)

❧❦❧

This seasoning will add to your culinary laurels if you don't limit it to *Sausage,* for this blend is sensational in *Meat Loaf* or *Balls, Veal, Roast Pork, Meat Pies, Biscuits,* and *Vegetable Fritters.*

If your butcher's Sausage is too fat for you or not seasoned to your taste, it's easy fun to make your own ten patties to go with the Breakfast Eggs or Waffles:

Ask the butcher to grind finely 1 pound of not-too-fat Pork Shoulder Meat. Take it home, and mix into it three or four (four for my taste), of this anthology of aromatics. Let the meat stand several hours—overnight is just right—before using. These are worth getting up for in the morning.

Although Pork isn't known for its long-keeping qualities, high seasoning helps prolong the quality of Pork Sausage. (In ages past when there was no refrigeration, spices were esteemed as much for their preservative power as for their flavors and fragrances.)

"Sausage-and-Other Seasoning" is a good way to remember this blend for which your spice sense will soon be suggesting still other uses.

My Favorite SAUSAGE SEASONING Recipe

ONION PIE

Line a pie pan with any standard Pastry. Fill with thinly sliced Bermuda Onions. Beat 2 eggs until very light, and add 1¼ cups Milk, ¼ teaspoon Salt, ¼ teaspoon Sausage Seasoning, 2 chopped strips of uncooked Bacon, and pour mixture over Onions. Bake 10 minutes at 450° F. Then reduce heat to 325°, and bake 30 minutes longer, or until Onions are tender.

This is an interesting variation from the usual vegetable dish.

SAVORY
(Herb)

A few Savory leaves in the cooking *Turnips* or *Cabbage* will reduce their strong cooking odors. Many cooks also drop a few of the leaves into the *Boiling Ham*—for flavor, of course. The English are especially fond of Savory for seasoning *Poultry*.

This Mint-family herb, which has a more delicate flavor than Sage, can be used in any way Sage is. In fact, it frequently goes in for Sage. This, "The Bean Herb," is an easy-to-grow spicy annual (but most of our supply comes from Spain and France) that is highly relished as a seasoning in *Bean, Pea,* and *Lentil* dishes.

A light dash of whole or ground Savory, which has a slightly resinous flavor reminiscent of Marjoram's, can pick up almost *any Meat* or *Vegetable Dish,* but more specifically these:

Vegetable, Bean, Split Pea, or *Lentil Soup;*

Horseradish Sauce, Butter Sauce for *Vegetables, Gravies;*

Chicken Croquettes, Ham, Hamburgers, Sausage, Stews, Mutton, Meat Balls or *Loaf, Liver Pastes, Stuffings, Turkey Turnovers, Rabbit, Fish* (especially *Boiled*);

Deviled or *Scrambled Eggs; Biscuits; Green Salads, Cole Slaws, Tomato* or *Potato Salads;*

Asparagus, Rice, Cucumbers, Cabbage, Cauliflower, Brussels Sprouts, Eggplant, Lima Beans, Squash, Green Beans, English Peas, Sauerkraut.

One of Savory's greatest virtues is its versatility in combining tastefully with other seasonings. (Savory is often combined with Pine Needles for stuffing pillows.)

Summer Savory and Winter Savory have similar flavors and are used in a similar manner, but Winter is much more pungent than Summer. Winter Savory is especially relished in *Egg Dishes, Poultry Stuffings* (this herb is in most Poultry Seasonings), *Broiled Fish, Potato Salad, French Dressings, Meat Sauces,* and *Fish Chowders.*

In short, if some dish seems flat, call on Savory. It will rise to the challenge, for Savory can make leftovers taste like firstovers.

My Favorite SAVORY Recipe

SAVORY BEAN SALAD

1 can Red Kidney Beans, washed and drained

4 ripe Tomatoes, chopped and drained

2 Green Peppers, chopped

½ teaspoon Salt

3 Boiled Eggs, chopped

2 cups finely shredded crisp Cabbage

1 cup chopped Celery

1 Bermuda Onion, minced

¼ teaspoon Savory

⅛ teaspoon Pepper

Combine ingredients, and moisten with Mayonnaise. Chill. Serve in Lettuce Cups.

the slaves called them Benneseed. The best of this fancy variety of these seed comes from Turkey, India, and China. The seeds are grown in DeLand, Florida.

Season Chicken Pie Crust with both in cooking and in making Pastry Tarts.

A third of the way around the world, fresh, whole Sesame Cakes are sold in the market places. Ground into flour, the Seed become bread . . . pressed, they become salad oil.

ڪئ

SESAME SEED
(Seed)

ڪئ

A picayune pinch of Sesame Seed in *Cream of Chicken Soup* will draw comments of delight. Two teaspoons of the Seed can give unctuous perfection to *Cheesecake—quel* cake! (Soft Cheesecake needs the texture bounce of these Seed.)

Perhaps most of us first heard of Sesame in "Ali Baba and the Forty Thieves." The hulled, pearly-white seed of this annual herb can be the "Open Sesame" to delicious *Cakes, Cookies, Confections, Cream Soups, Cheeses, Salads, Biscuits, Crumpets, Scones, Rice, Potatoes, Noodles, Fish, Chicken Pie Crust,* and *Crumb Toppings* for *Casseroles.*

The flavor of baked Sesame Seed is surprisingly like that of toasted almonds. Use these seed in any way nuts are used. The ancients used them to enrich their *Bread* and *Cakes.*

Tons of the minute seed (they're about ⅛" long) are used each year to make *Halvah,* a delicious Turkish Candy. Sesame Seed *Brittle* is a novelty confection made in the Great Smoky Mountains for the tourist trade.

Orientals still use ground Sesame Seed as a food much as the ancient Egyptians and Persians did. Legend holds that Yama, "God of Death," created Sesame. The Seed were once used in funeral rites as a symbol of immortality; to Brahmins the Seed still signify immortality.

This annual, a native of Asia, may be grown from either seed or cuttings. Negro slaves first brought Sesame Seed to America;

the slaves called them Beneseed. The best of the fancy orange variety of these seed comes from Turkey, India, and China. The seed are available hulled or unhulled.

Sesame Oil, a gourmet item, is used both in *cooking* and in making *Salad Dressings*.

A myth of the early Assyrians who lived thousands of years Before Christ holds that their gods drank Sesame Wine at their conference prior to creating the earth.

Sesame Seed helped one cook begin 1955 $25,000 richer. She used these savories in her *Open Sesame Pie* which won first place in a national bake-off. Your next *Chicken Cutlets* will be rich prizes if you add Sesame Seed to their crumb coating.

My Favorite SESAME SEED Recipe

SESAME CLOVER ROLLS
(No Yeast)

2 cups sifted all-purpose Flour	½ cup Milk
¾ teaspoon Soda	3 tablespoons fresh or bottled
½ teaspoon Salt	Lemon Juice
1 tablespoon Sugar	2 tablespoons Sesame Seed for
⅓ cup Shortening	sprinkling tops of rolls

Sift dry ingredients together, and cut shortening into them until like coarse corn meal. Combine the Milk and Lemon Juice, and add to first mixture. Stir quickly to form a soft dough. Knead lightly, and form into balls the size of large marbles. Place 3 balls in each greased muffin tin. Sprinkle tops of rolls generously with Sesame Seed. Bake 20 minutes at 450° F.

≈ଟ୍ରକ≈

SHALLOTS *or* ESCHALOTS
(Herb)

≈ଟ୍ରକ≈

This delicately-flavored Onionlike plant is used much as Onions **are** to give lip-smacking savor to:

Halibut, Cod, Whitefish; Broiled Steak, Veal Chops, Duck, Rabbit, Kidney, Stews, Liver, Poultry; Butter Sauces (Shallots are especially popular for seasoning sauces).

When sautéing Shallots, never allow them to brown, for that gives them a bitter taste.

These reddish-brown bulbs, which are bachelor-popular in European cookery, have a more subtle flavor than Onions, a flavor that can give extra goodness to many different dishes.

Shallots are not always easily available. Look for them in the **bigger** markets. Use Shallots as a substitute for Onion or Garlic.

✤❧ ✤

SMOKE FLAVOR
(Condiment)

✤❧✤

This outdoorsy essence gives a seemingly genuine Smoke flavor
to:

Hamburgers, Roasts, Steaks, Chops, Lamb, Spareribs, Fowl; Fish; Barbecue Sauces; Black Bean or Pea Soup; Gumbos; Egg Dishes; Canapé Spreads; Baked Beans and other *Vegetable Dishes.*

Smoke Flavor, which is made of refined condensed Wood
Smoke Concentrate, Caramel, Vinegar, Tomatoes, Salt, Vegetable Protein Derivatives, and Spices, is recommended highly for
giving a real barbecue taste to oven-prepared Meats. The flavor
will penetrate the Meat more thoroughly if the seasoning is
brushed on the Meat several hours before cooking time.

Smoke Flavor is said to have made the barbecue pit antique!

My Favorite SMOKE FLAVOR Recipe

BRAISED BEEF FOR COLD CUTS OR SANDWICHES

The following method will give moist tender "Roast" Beef that will
not dry out when held over for later serving. (Cooked by dry heat,
even a choice Sirloin Tip will dry out when held over.)

Rub Roast with Smoke Flavor at least 3 hours before cooking
time, and let stand at room temperature. Sear the unfloured Roast in

a very hot preheated heavy roaster (or a heavy skillet with a close-fitting lid, for later use). When Roast is well-browned on all sides, reduce heat as low as possible, and place top on roaster. (Add no water or other seasonings.) Cook as slowly as possible 2 to 4 hours, depending on size and quality of Roast. About 45 minutes before done, season the Roast with Salt, Pepper, and Onions, if desired. (Carrots and Potatoes may also be placed with roast to cook.) Continue cooking until Meat is tender and the Vegetables, if any, done.

Remove Meat from juices while still warm, and place in a covered casserole. When cool, refrigerate. Also cool and refrigerate juices; later remove layer of fat from top. This stock makes delicious natural or thickened gravy.

SORREL
(Herb)

❧❦❧

Sorrel soup, an Old English concoction, is still served today. In England the sour flavor of Sorrel is also popular served with *Mutton* or *Beef*.

This perennial, which is grown from seed, has a Lemonlike tang. Its young, tender leaves are used both as *Cooked Greens* and as a seasoning for other foods, especially:

Green Salads, Mixed Cooked Greens (usually with *Spinach* or *Cabbage*); *Soups; Scrambled Eggs* and *Omelets; Fish*.

Garniture chiffonade, a garnish for *Consommés,* is made by parboiling finely-shredded Sorrel in boiling, lightly-salted water for 1 minute. The Sorrel is then drained and placed in the *Consommé* just before it is served.

❧❧❧

SOY SAUCE
(Condiment)

❧❧❧

On Chop Suey, Chow Mein, and other Chinese food, yes, but do you know what this hearty sauce will do for—

Chops, Roasts, Stews, and *Gravies?*

A *soupçon* of this liquid luxury in the batter for *Vegetable* or *Meat Fritters* will make mysteriously good fritters.

Here's a chef caper with this concoction of fermented soybeans, salt, and secret spices: Marinate *Steaks* in Soy Sauce for 1 hour before broiling them. Oo-la-la!

Broiling, I said, but I'd just as soon slap them down tightly on a HOT ungreased skillet. The Steaks are accommodating; they'll loosen when ready to be turned. When both sides are browned, the Steaks go on hot plates, and a bit of scalding water goes into the brown-crusted skillet. (Enough Soy Sauce there to give the natural gravy a delicious flavor and a rich color.) A wooden spoon does a hushed job of loosening every tasty brown particle. Each person salts his own Steak, for Soy Sauce is *salty*.

The best *Baked Spareribs* I ever tasted were seasoned with a combination of Soy Sauce, Garlic, Dry Mustard, and a little Honey. Bake at 300° F. 2½ hours.

TABASCO SAUCE
(Condiment)

This HOT sauce can give plenty of flavor-fire to *Green Beans, Dried Beans, Black-Eyed Peas, Cabbage, Turnips, Squash, Mixed Greens, Black Bean Soup, Creamed Chicken, Seafoods,* and *Sauces.*

Use a drop or two of Tabasco Sauce in *Creamed Egg* or *Cheese Dishes,* especially in *Macaroni and Cheese.*

This saucy sauce is named after the Mexican state of Tabasco where *capsicum annum,* the principal ingredient of the condiment, is grown. However, there are numerous "Tabasco" sauces, red-hot sauces of similar flavor, which are marketed under various brand names.

My Favorite TABASCO SAUCE Recipe

CHEESE STRATA

1 dozen slices day-old Bread	¼ teaspoon Worcestershire
½ pound grated sharp Cheddar	Sauce
4 Eggs, beaten very light	¼ teaspoon Onion Salt
3 cups Milk	Butter or Margarine for
¼ teaspoon Tabasco Sauce	spreading Bread
¼ teaspoon Marjoram	

Butter the day-old Bread (fresh Bread will be gummy for this use), and make Sandwiches of the Buttered Bread and the grated Cheese.

Place Sandwiches in a well-greased shallow pan. Add the beaten Eggs to the Milk, and stir in the Seasonings. Pour mixture over Sandwiches. Cover, and let stand in refrigerator 24 hours before using. Then bake at 300° F. about 50 minutes. Cheese Strata will be puffed and golden when done. Serve promptly with Bacon Strips or Grilled Ham.

TANSY
(Herb)

A "Tansy" is a Tansy-tinctured *Baked Custard* of English origin. *Tansy Cakes* for Easter are an English custom.

The tender, bitter green leaves of young Tansy plants are used cautiously to season:

Beef Pies, Lamb Stew, Stuffings for Poultry and Veal; *Baked Fish* (Izaak Walton suggested Tansy with Fish); *Omelets; Green Salads; Custards* and *Puddings*.

This perennial, which can be grown either from seed or root division, once signified immortality. Tansy *Tea* is another of the old-time home remedies.

❦❦❦

TARRAGON
(Herb)

❦❦❦

Tarragon *Vinegar* is a jump-ahead starting point for the young cook. It gives a royal touch to *Green* or *Seafood Salads.*

Here's how to make it: Place 1 tablespoon dried Tarragon in 1 pint Wine Vinegar, and cover. Let it stand a week, and then strain and bottle. You can begin with Tarragon Vinegar in *Mashed Potatoes,* or *Avocado Dip,* but don't limit yourself to a beginning.

Tarragon's aromatic flavor, which is reminiscent of Anise, stands well alone, although it must be used lightly. Tarragon, whole or ground, can enhance the tastiness of any nonsweet food. Take your pick:

Pickles; Lobster, Salmon, Tuna Fish, and other *Seafoods.* (Tarragon and Cucumber are always jostling for the Seafood honor), including *Chowders;*

Veal, Squab, Duck, Pheasant, Broiled Chicken, Goose, Rabbit, Steaks, Meat Aspics;

Green Peas, Celery, Spinach, Beets, Broccoli, Cooked Greens, Artichokes, Cauliflower, Tomatoes, Mushrooms, Asparagus, Cabbage, Vegetable Juices;

Deviled or *Scrambled Eggs* and *Omelets; Tartar* and *Butter Sauces; Cottage Cheese, Cheese Dishes; Cream of Mushroom, Turtle,* or *Tomato Soup.*

With a little Tarragon in it, *Chicken à la King* becomes fit for a king.

Unlike most other herbs, Tarragon is not so pungent dried as when fresh. This perennial, one native to Western Asia, is grown from cuttings, not seed.

Tarragon's long slender leaves often appear as a garnish on Aspic-covered Meats. The French, from whom we import much of this herb, especially favor Tarragon for this purpose. The Persians favor nibbling the pungent fresh leaves as an *Appetizer*.

Brussels Sprouts, pickled in Tarragon Vinegar for serving as a relish on the Tray of Cold Cuts, or with Roast Beef, are a gastronome's creation.

My Favorite TARRAGON Recipe

TUNA FISH SALAD (CONGEALED)
(25 Servings)

Since this Salad is especially appropriate for entertaining it is given in quantity size; however, it can easily be reduced one-fourth to serve six.

Soften 5 envelopes Plain Gelatin in 1 cup Cold Water, and set aside. Combine the following ingredients, and cook in double boiler until thick, stirring constantly:

5 Eggs, beaten light	1 teaspoon Paprika
1 cup rich Milk	5 tablespoons Flour
1½ teaspoons Salt	6 tablespoons Sugar
1 tablespoon Dry Mustard	1 cup Tarragon Vinegar

Stir 2½ cups hot water into mixture, and cook until smooth. Add the softened Gelatin. Let cool until mixture begins to thicken, and then add:

1 teaspoon grated Onion	½ cup finely chopped Sweet Pickle
1 cup finely chopped Celery	
1 tablespoon finely minced Parsley	2 Pimientos, finely chopped
4 cans drained, flaked Tuna Fish	

Pour into individual molds that have been brushed lightly with Salad Oil. Chill until firm. Unmold on Shredded Lettuce. Garnish with Mayonnaise and a Pimiento-Stuffed Olive.

THYME
(Herb)

❧❧❧

A wee bit of Thyme in *Melted Butter* or *Margarine* for topping *Hot Vegetables* is a Thymely tip for one Vegetable at each meal. Thyme is also compatible with *Meats*.

French chefs depend on Thyme as the lead flavor in their *bouquet garni*.

If Sicily's delicacy *Thyme Honey* isn't easily available to you, here's another that is: Thyme dusted lightly on your *Tomato Salad*. Izaak Walton, himself, noted that Thyme and *Fish* go together.

Thyme's Mintlike flavor is just as heavenly as its fragrance (which Kipling said was like the perfume of the dawn of Paradise), when used with a fairy touch, especially in *Veal* or *Pork*.

The Persians once nibbled fresh Thyme as an appetizer. (Some ancients thought Thyme gave one courage). Today Louisiana cooks are enthusiastic over the hearty flavor Thyme gives to many of their dishes.

Garden or Common Thyme, which grows easily from seed or cuttings, is the variety generally used in cookery, although there are many types of this Mint-family perennial. Much Thyme is grown in America, but a large quantity is also imported from France and Spain.

The fresh or dried leaves of this herb can also be used, whole or powdered, to give new appeal to:

Green Salads, Cottage Cheese Salads;

Split Pea or *Vegetable Soup, Oyster Stew, Clam Juice, Clam Chowder* (*Manhattan Clam Chowder* is dependent on Thyme's touch), *Gumbos, Borscht; Seafood Cocktail Sauces;*

Cheese or *Egg Dishes;*

Beef Stew, Corned Beef Hash, Poultry, Meat Loaf, Baked Fish, Lamb, Fish Balls, Roast Beef (especially), *Veal, Pork,* any *Meat Stuffing;*

Green Beans or *Peas, Tomatoes, Eggplant, Carrots, Spinach, Onions, Beets, Potatoes, Broiled Green Tomatoes.*

A blend of Thyme, Rosemary, and Marjoram is preferred by many cooks for seasoning *Poultry Stuffings;* those cooks consider the usual Sage too heavy for Chicken and Turkey.

Thyme mixes unusually well with other milder-flavored herbs. Many an old family recipe calls for "a sprig of Thyme." That means a half-teaspoon of today's powdered Thyme.

When King Charlemagne called herbs "the praise of cooks," he could easily have been thinking of tasty Thyme, even though this herb wasn't widely used in the cookery of his time.

My Favorite THYME Recipe

THYMELY GREEN BEAN CASSEROLE

Melt ¼ cup Butter or Margarine, and blend into it ¼ cup Flour. Stir into it gradually 2 cups hot liquid (Bean liquid, Chicken Broth, etc.) Season to taste with Salt and Pepper, and add ¼ teaspoon Thyme, ½ teaspoon Dry Mustard, ¼ teaspoon Worcestershire Sauce. Cool mixture. Then fold into the Sauce 3 chopped Pimientos, ½ cup chopped Celery, ½ cup grated sharp Cheddar, and 1 can drained French-cut String Beans. Pour mixture into a greased casserole, top with Buttered Crumbs, and bake 30 minutes at 350° or until Crumbs are browned.

᪥ᨠᨠᨠᨦ

TOMATO PRODUCTS

᪥ᨠᨠᨠᨦ

Good as fresh Tomatoes are, it's much easier to use some canned form of them as a seasoning; and sometimes the canned product is even tastier.

Use any Tomato product at all to add flavor- and color-richness to *Meat Loaf, Meat Balls, Cheese Dishes, Egg Dishes, Spaghetti Sauce, Rice Dishes, Stews, Soups, Sauces, Gravies, Fish,* and *Vegetable Dishes.*

Tomato can often renovate both the flavor and the color of a leftover food to help it make a successful comeback.

Tomato Sauce is seasoned Tomato pulp, usually packed in an eight-ounce can. Use it just as it comes from the can for saucing *Hamburgers, Croquettes,* and other *Meat Dishes,* or use it as an ingredient in preparing any Tomato-flavored dish.

Tomato Paste is an unseasoned, strained paste, which is favored for making *Sauces.* This product is usually packed in a six-ounce can.

Tomato Puree is very similar to Paste, but the Puree is salted and often has a little more water content than the Paste. Puree, which comes in a 10½-ounce or larger can, is most often used as a *Soup* or *Sauce Base.*

Condensed Cream of Tomato Soup is a well-seasoned concentrate that is highly versatile. This Soup can be used as a delicious Sauce when diluted with ⅓ cup Milk. An unusually good, long-keeping French Dressing can be made from the Soup.

Tomato Juice or *Canned Tomatoes* are often used as an important ingredient in foods, but for seasoning use I have found that these add a more acid taste to food than do the other Tomato products.

Tomato Catsup is a seedless condiment that is well-flavored with Vinegar, Spices, Onion, Garlic, and Sugar. It makes an excellent short-cut seasoning for *Barbecue Sauces.* With added Horseradish and finely-chopped Celery, Catsup makes a delicious *Seafood Cocktail Sauce.* Catsup, which usually comes in a 14-ounce bottle, should be kept refrigerated when not in use.

Chili Sauce is even better than Catsup for seasoning use. The Tomato Seed which are left in Chili Sauce give it additional flavor. This Sauce is often used in making *French Dressing,* a type that has good body and good looks, to go over *Cole Slaw.* As the name implies this condiment includes Chili Peppers in its makeup.

There are so many good Tomato Products to choose from it is sometimes difficult to decide just which one is really ideal for *Meat Loaf,* which for *Spaghetti Sauce,* and so on. It's comforting to realize that any Tomato Product can be adapted to substitute for another.

My Favorite TOMATO CATSUP Recipe

BARBECUE SAUCE FOR CHICKEN

Mix the following ingredients together and simmer 30 minutes:

2 cups Butter or Margarine	¼ teaspoon Cayenne
2 cups Water	1 tablespoon Worcestershire
1 cup Vinegar	Sauce
1 cup Catsup	1 tablespoon Tabasco Sauce
2 teaspoons Dry Mustard	1 tablespoon Black Pepper
2 tablespoons Brown Sugar	1 medium Onion, minced
1½ tablespoons each Salt, Chili Powder, Paprika	1 Clove of Garlic, minced

Baste broiling Chickens with Sauce every 5 minutes until tender, about 50 minutes.

❧❦❧

TRUFFLES

❧❦❧

". . . Musky, fiery, savoury, mysterious—a hot, drousy smell, that lulls the senses, and yet enflames them . . ." is the tantalizing description a Thackeray quote gives of the aroma of Truffles, the most sophisticated of seasonings.

The prized black Truffles, often called "black pearls," are a finely marbled black throughout; they grow chiefly in France. Périqueux, France, is "The Truffle Capital of the World." A white type of Truffle comes from North Africa and Italy; some Truffles come from Germany. In color, Truffles may also be chocolate brown or reddish brown.

Dogs have been trained to hunt Truffles, which grow from six inches to four feet underground. Truffle hunters also follow their pigs about during the November-to-February harvesting season and snatch the fragrant fungi-fruit from their disappointed swine as they uproot the morsels. (There are said to be a few trained pig Trufflers!) Truffles range up to the size of an orange, but the walnut-sized ones are reported to be the best flavored.

Truffles have always been a mystery to man. Pliny, the great Roman naturalist and author, who lived from A.D. 23 to 79, thought them Mother Nature's most marvelous, mysterious creation. Other wise men have thought these delicacies, which have no stems or roots, to be created by thunder (Theophrastus believed this), also declaring they grow only in areas that have wet springs, hot summers with frequent thunderstorms, and cool autumns.

The morsels are found in poor soil and, some hunters say, near a certain kind of oak tree, called "Truffle Oak." Usually nothing else grows in the immediate vicinity of Truffles, and finding them in a certain spot one season doesn't necessarily mean they will be there next season. Truffles have resisted all man's efforts to grow them.

These aromatics have been respected for their culinary capabilities for centuries, although in France they came into favor and went out a number of times. These delicacies have also been valued for their aphrodisiac qualities; Pythagoras, the Greek philosopher, recommended them to a childless friend.

Today gourmets and chefs the world over prize Truffles as a tasty garnish, an exquisitely-flavored food, and as a fragrant seasoning. The French relish them in or on *Poultry, Meats, Cold Liver Pastes* (especially in *paté de fois gras*), *Cheese Dishes, Duck* (France's traditional Roast Duck for Christmas is Truffled), *Sausage, Ragouts, Sauces, Seafood,* and *Vegetable Dishes*. Brillat-Savarin called Truffles "Black diamonds of the *haute cuisine*." The crisp morsels are sliced paper-thin; in fact, a Truffle slicer is a gadget that holds a standard safety razor blade. No part of a Truffle is discarded; even the peel can embellish omelets.

Due to their scarcity, Truffles have always been and will probably continue to be an epicurean item. But everyone should experience them at least once and then bask in the memory of the dark delights.

TURMERIC
(Spice)

Turmeric, like Dill, has been too long banished to the Pickle jar. This spice, which is popular in East Indian cookery, can complement the natural good flavor of *Broiled Chicken; Creamed Egg Dishes; Rice Dishes; Cream Sauces* for Meat and Fish; *Pickles, Relishes, Chowchows, Prepared Mustard; Cakes* and *Cookies; Salad Dressings.*

Turmeric gives the gold to Curry Powder. (A little additional Turmeric improves Curried *Veal, Beef,* or *Mutton.*) This ground rootstock of a Ginger-family plant is also used as a dye. (Turmeric was known as a perfume in Biblical times.) In cookery, colorful Turmeric often pinchhits for expensive Saffron.

The new Turmeric user can make cautious acquaintance with this seasoning by adding a bit of it to the *French Dressing* for a salad of Tomatoes and Avocados. Or by adding a teaspoon of it to the next bowl of *Mayonnaise.* With Turmeric's help Mayonnaise never looks anemic.

My Favorite TURMERIC Recipe

MAYONNAISE

Beat 2 Egg Yolks until very light, and add to them:

1 teaspoon Turmeric	1 teaspoon Dry Mustard
½ teaspoon Salt	1 tablespoon Lemon Juice

Add, a drop or so at a time to start with, 1 pint Salad Oil, beating constantly. When the mixture begins to emulsify the Oil may be added much faster. When half the Oil is used, add 1 tablespoon Vinegar. After beating in the remaining Oil, check the Salt. Then beat in as quickly as possible 2 tablespoons Boiling Water. (This helps kill the raw egg taste and also helps keep the dressing from turning back to Oil should the Mayonnaise become too cold in the refrigerator.)

VANILLA
(Spice)

Vanilla is truly the orchid among flavorings. It is first in our national taste. (Lemon is second.)

The flowers of the *Vanilla planifolia,* a member of the orchid family, turn into flavorful, bean-filled pods, which may be used in their natural form (dried) as a flavoring. When Vanilla Bean is used it is often steeped in a little hot milk to extract its flavor. (One inch of Vanilla Bean will flavor Custard for four servings.) Extract, however, is the more popular form of Vanilla.

Candies, Baked Products, all *Sweet Dishes*—and even perfumes—make generous use of this Extract. (Not too many generations back, the fragrance of pure Vanilla Extract wafted from many feminine churchgoers.)

A drop of this exotic essence adds an almost indistinguishable aroma to the gourmet's *Hot Cakes.* (Two drops are one too many.)

A combination of Vanilla and Almond Extracts equals pistachio flavor. A mock one, to be sure, but good.

My Favorite VANILLA Recipe

OLD-FASHIONED "BOILED" CUSTARD

2 quarts Milk, scalded	1 cup Sugar
6 whole Eggs, slightly beaten	¼ teaspoon Salt

1 tablespoon Vanilla

Add scalded Milk slowly to Eggs and Sugar and Salt. Cook over hot water only until Custard will coat a silver spoon. ("Boiled," of course, is a misnomer, for this dessert-drink must never boil or it will curdle.) Remove from heat at once. Cool. Pour Custard into a large pitcher and chill before serving. Serve in juice glasses for dessert or refreshment, topping each glass with Whipped Cream.

VINEGAR

Nose-tickling *Vinegar Pudding* was a childhood delight. *Chess Tarts* still rely on Vinegar's acidity for flavor interest. Acetic acid gives Vinegar its characteristic sour taste.

There are Malt and Beer, Cider and other fruit, Wine, and imitation Vinegars. In flavor Vinegars may range from delicate to robust. Good Cider Vinegar, incidentally, has the tantalizing fragrance of Apples. Cheap Vinegar is cheap Vinegar.

Wine Vinegars, which are most popular in fine cookery, are made from either Red or White Wines. These are less acid-tasting than other Vinegars. Although there's little difference between the flavors of Red and White Wine Vinegars, the Red looks more provocative. *Fresh Vegetables* and *Cooked Greens* blossom under the touch of Wine Vinegar.

Vinegars may be flavored with many things, including herbs, spices, Woods Violets, and Nasturtiums.

Mellow Herb-Flavored Vinegars (which can be made from any type Vinegar) are used to season the same foods in which the herbs themselves are often used, but such Vinegars are greatly valued for making *Salad Dressings*. It's easy to make your own flavored vinegars from either fresh or dried herbs:

1. *Fresh Herbs*: Place 2 cups minced fresh herb leaves in a quart of good vinegar, and let jar stand in a warm place two weeks, shaking the mixture every day or so. Then strain, bottle, and seal.

2. *Dried Herbs or Aromatic Seeds*: Use 1½ tablespoons dried

herbs or 1½ ounces of seeds to a quart of *scalded* vinegar, and then follow above procedure.

Vinegar is most often used to give gustatory goodness to:

Cabbage, Turnips, Mixed Greens, Mushrooms, Artichokes, Mashed Potatoes;
Deviled Eggs; Fish; Potato Salad; Seafoods; Green Salads;
Salad Dressings; Soups; Gravies; Sauces.

And to *tenderize* and flavor *Steaks* and *Roasts* by marinating the Meat in a Vinegar-and-Oil mixture for several hours before cooking. (See MARINADE.)

My Favorite VINEGAR Recipe

CHESS PIES
(20 4″ Tarts)

Collecting Chess Pie Recipes has been one of my minor hobbies. I consider these the most elegant Chess Pies I have ever seen or tasted. The recipe was developed by Mrs. T. L. Huddleston of Murfreesboro, Tennessee, from a much older version that had long been in her family.

8 Egg Yolks	Juice of 1 Lemon
2 cups Sugar	½ cup Cream
1 tablespoon Vinegar	1½ sticks Butter
2 tablespoons Corn Meal	

Cream Butter and Sugar very light, and then beat in Yolks one at a time. Blend in other ingredients. Bake in individual pie pans lined with pastry, at 300° F. until centers are just set.

(The uncooked filling may be kept for several days in a covered jar in the refrigerator, but let filling come to room temperature before using.)

VIOLETS

Vinegar for use in Fruit Salad Dressings is sometimes flavored with Violets, but Violets' favorite culinary role is as a dainty tidbit in the form of *Candied Violets*. Some specialty houses market these, but many cook-hostesses make their own by brushing the clean, fresh blossoms with Egg White and then sprinkling well with finely granulated Sugar. The blossoms are then allowed to dry. When dry they are stored between sheets of waxed paper in air-tight containers. These confections make unusual gifts.

Tender green violet leaves have long been mixed with other *Salad Greens*. The chopped leaves also appear in *Omelets*. And then there is the *Violet Blossom Salad*—on which only my eyes could feast.

<svg>decorative ornament</svg>

WATER CHESTNUTS

<svg>decorative ornament</svg>

Chinese cookery uses Water Chestnuts in a great many ways. A good habit of the cosmopolitan cook is using these canned Chestnuts to give a crisp texture contrast to *Creamed Dishes, Tossed Green Salads,* and *Fruit Salads.* Chestnuts' crunchiness offsets the mushiness of salads made from Canned Fruits.

Water Chestnuts have been observed, Bacon-wrapped and broiled, stealing the conversational spotlight on the hors-d'oeuvres tray. Another habit the hostess will find worth cultivating. Whatever Chestnuts' role, guests sit up and take notice of them.

WATER CRESS

Craving for something different? Whip up a *Water Cress Omelet* and enjoy it while the narrator narrates . . .

This most ancient of green vegetables known to man can be traced back to the Persians, the Greeks, and the Romans. Sprays of Water Cress were nibbled as finger food as the first course at Roman banquets. Xerxes recommended this green for improving the health of his soldiers (although nothing was known about vitamins and minerals then). Today Water Cress can also improve our cuisine.

This beautiful plant is always welcome as a graceful *garnish,* but it can also add a piquant flavor to foods—to *Biscuits, Cheese* and *Egg Dishes, Meats, Shellfish, Hors-d'Oeuvres, Cooked Mixed Greens,* and many other foods.

Water Cress can work tasty, colorful wonders with *Rice, Macaroni, Noodles,* and other pasty-looking foods. Just mince a bunch of the green leaves (save those stems for the *Salad Bowl* or *Soup Pot*) and fold them into the hot cooked food just before serving it.

Minced Water Cress leaves in the *Butter Sauce* for *Steamed Cauliflower* give a chef's touch. (Add the coarsely chopped leaves to the melted Butter just before serving.)

As a green on which to place other Salads, glossy Water Cress is unusually attractive and flavorful (quite peppery), but it does not hold up as long as lettuce. (Nor does lettuce hold up as long as that charm baby spinach.) Always leave Water Cress in the refrigerator until the last possible second. Immediately after getting this green home from the market, wash it, blot dry carefully, and store in covered containers in the refrigerator. Each day take a moment to remove any yellowing leaves that may have appeared.

A resourceful, last-century New Jersey lad is to be thanked for today's bountiful supply of Water Cress. Frank Dennis began picking wild Water Cress about ten years after the Civil War and peddling the green to his neighbors. Soon New York hotels and restaurants were using this plant in such quantity the boy had to start his own Water Cress farms to meet the demand. Today that business which began as a pin money activity supplies Water Cress to forty-four states.

This green, which was native to Europe and Asia, has beautifully shaped, bright green leaves and grows in sparkling running water. A tiny Water Cress bouquet makes a cunning garnish: Place three short sprigs of Water Cress around a Radish Rose, and tuck the "bouquet" through a Pickle Ring. A pretty trio.

The French make a delicious thick soup of Water Cress and Potatoes, called *Potage Cressonière*. The English made the *Water Cress Tea Sandwich* famous. (The late King George and Queen Elizabeth were served a *Water Cress* and *Frozen Cheese Salad* at the White House banquet given for them in 1939.) The Italians often use Water Cress in their hearty *Minestrone*. The Chinese use the green in their *Egg Drop* and *Won Ton*. The Germans have many uses for this green which they have grown since 1550. In America, we like to serve it much as the Romans did, with *garum,* or Oil and Vinegar. The Romans also served Water Cress with Pepper and Cummin Seed and Lentiscus.

The original *Oysters Rockefeller* were first prepared with this green that is rich in Vitamins A and C and also calcium and iron. Spinach finally replaced that use of it, probably because at one time Spinach was more readily available than Water Cress.

But that is no longer the case, for Water Cress has now come into its own.

My Favorite WATER CRESS Recipe

AVOCADO AND WATER CRESS SALAD

Place peeled Avocado Halves that have been drenched in Lemon Juice on a generous bed of Water Cress sprigs. Fill centers of Avocados with chilled Chili Sauce containing minced Shrimp, Horseradish, and finely chopped Celery. Garnish top with a whole Shrimp and the side of the plate with a Radish Rose.

242   WATER CRESS

But due to no longer this case. Pa, Water Cress has now come
into its own.

❧❧❧

WINE

❧❧❧

"To make a success of any dish, add Wine to the ingredients," **a**
famous French chef once advised. To make a success of your
next party dessert, stir a little Sherry into *Hot Mincemeat* and
spoon it over Vanilla Ice Cream. Oh, *mes amis,* what a *différence!*

Wine does belong in our kitchens just as much as Pepper,
Vanilla, and the other ingredients we use to pep up food. In
addition to being a thrifty seasoning (most seasonings sell by the
ounce, but Wine sells by the bottle). Wine is one of the best
all-around seasonings, too, for it's a culinary charmer in practically *any* dish—whether braised, baked, boiled, fricasséed,
creamed, or uncooked.

Although Sherry is the most popular of all wines for use in
cookery, *any* kind of Wine makes a superlative seasoning. Every
Cook needs to know the five types of Wines:

1. Appetizer Wines: Sherry and Vermouth. (Sherry can
range from sweet to dry; the sweet ones are dessert or refreshment wines. Vermouth is most frequently used in mixing Cocktails.)

2. Red Table Wines: Burgundy and Claret family Wines.

3. White Table Wines: Sauterne and Rhine Wine family
Wines.

4. Dessert Wines: Port, Tokay, Cream Sherry, Muscatel, etc.

5. All-Purpose Sparkling Wines: Champagne and Sparkling
Burgundy. (We prize these elegant Wines so much as beverages

they are seldom used in cooking, except by the most extravagant gourmets.)

Only the best Wine should be used in cooking, as for drinking. The "cooking" Sherries found in some supermarkets are lacking in flavor.

"Red Wines in dark foods, white Wines in light foods," is the long established "rule." But that is only a starting point for the imaginative cook; after becoming familiar with some of the accepted affinities she will want to experiment on her own, even using White Wines in *dark foods,* and vice versa. As in using other seasonings, the Wine cook is a rule unto herself, for she aims only to combine those Food and Wine flavors that are delightful to *her* taste.

Wine's flavor in food is indescribably different and amazingly delicious. Here are a few of the accepted affinities:

soups: *Clear*: Add 1 tablespoon of Red Wine (perhaps Burgundy) or of Dry Vermouth to each cup just before serving. *Cream*: Add Sherry to these. Wine should be added to *Soups, Gravies, Sauces,* etc., just before removing them from the heat, for Wine should not be boiled. (Wine's light flavor is overwhelmed in heavy *Vegetable Soup*.)

fruit: *Melon Balls, Fruit Cups, Pears, Peaches, Grapes,* etc., to be served either as appetizers or desserts become something special when accented with White Tokay, Sherry, or other Wine. Add the Wine about three hours before serving time, and chill the fruit.

vegetables: All Vegetables, except strong-tasting ones like Turnips, Green Peppers, and Onions, become outstanding when given the flavor brilliance of a bit of Wine, along with the other usual seasonings. *Green Peas, Carrots,* etc., like the light White Wines, while the darker dishes such as *Tomatoes, Kidney Beans, Baked Beans,* etc., respond to the full-bodied Red Wines.

meat, fish, poultry: Baste any baking or roasting *Meat*

with Wine. *Lamb* or *Veal* likes a White Wine such as Sauterne. *Beef* or *Ham* prefer Sherry or a Red Wine like Burgundy. *Fish* like to swim in Dry Vermouth.

Wine is often used as a Marinade (see *Marinade*) in *Meat* cookery. One or two cups are poured over the Meat which is then allowed to stand several hours before cooking. The Meat is turned occasionally to let the Wine penetrate it to tenderize and flavor the Meat. Left-over Marinade can be used for basting or gravy-making. A Wine Marinade on an inexpensive cut of Meat for pot roasting proves Wine's worth as a seasoning.

Chicken, Shrimp, Crab Meat, and *Lobsters* make extra deluxe salads if first marinated in a little White Wine, perhaps Sauterne or Rhine Wine, before being mixed with other ingredients.

DESSERTS: A sweet Dessert Wine, like Port or Muscatel, spooned over *Ice Cream, Hot Puddings, Broiled Grapefruit,* etc., is a joy to even the most pampered palate.

Wine does two things to food: It adds its own delicate bouquet as a flavor (which may be nutty, fruity, tangy, or tart), and it also blends the flavors of the other ingredients in a food. Incidentally, the alcohol in Wine evaporates during the cooking process as it does from Vanilla. Used with a light touch (a tablespoon or two to each serving of food) Wine can glamorize any food. Two tablespoons of Sherry in your next *Baked Beans* will sell you on Wine as a seasoning.

My Favorite WINE Recipe

BURGUNDY CAKE

3 tablespoons Plain Gelatin, softened in ¼ cup Cold Water	1¼ cups Orange Juice
	1 tablespoon Lemon Juice
	1½ cups Burgundy
¾ cup Sugar	Red Food Coloring
⅛ teaspoon Salt	1 Sponge Cake
¾ cup Hot Water	1 pint Whipping Cream

Dissolve the softened gelatin in the hot water. Add Sugar, and stir until dissolved. Let mixture cool. Add other ingredients, including a few drops of Red Food Coloring if needed to make the mixture a good color. Chill Gelatin until slightly thickened. Hollow out a Sponge Cake, leaving both bottom and sides rather thick, and fill with Gelatin. Frost Cake with Whipped Cream. Chill thoroughly before serving.

WOODRUFF
(Herb)

❧❦❧

This sweet-smelling perennial is used most frequently to give a fragrant fillip to *Wine Cups* (especially *Champagne*), *Lemonade, Fruit Punches,* and *Fruit Cups. Maibowle* is a German beverage made by steeping Woodruff sprigs in Rhine Wine.

‧⁌§§⁍‧

WORCESTERSHIRE SAUCE
(Condiment)

‧⁌§§⁍‧

This murky, mysterious sauce, we are told, has over one hundred ingredients in it! Well, let's see . . . Onions, Tamarinds, Garlic, Salt, Sugar, Caramel, Eschalots, Lime Juice, Malt Vinegar, Anchovies, and many spices!

Whatever is in it, this brisk black-brown liquid that flows from days of antiquity can pique the most bored palate.

Men especially like to dash this "steak" sauce onto *Lamb Chops, Meat Balls,* and *Steaks,* but this robust condiment plays an even more important role in the kitchen. The sauce can do wonderful things to *Meat Dishes, Seafood, Egg Dishes,* and *Cheese Casseroles.* Since a dash is potent the careful cook dashes and tastes and repeats until her tasting spoon approves.

A variety of this sauce is made in Worcester, England, from which city it gets its name; however, this condiment originated in ancient days. American versions of it carry a variety of names, but most of the sauces have a similar flavor.

A dash of Worcestershire can stiffen the backbone of *Tomato Juice,* making it a zesty cocktail. *Macaroni* and *Cheese* comes up lacking when without this seasoning. And, with Worcestershire Sauce blended in it, any *Roquefort Cheese Dressing* instantly becomes famous. Meat sauce or no, many a well-dressed *Salad* wears a dash of Worcestershire Sauce.

My Favorite WORCESTERSHIRE SAUCE Recipe

THE OLD RED ROOSTER

1 Rooster or Hen, cut up as for frying	1 tablespoon Worcestershire Sauce
1 cup diced Celery	1 tablespoon Parsley Flakes
¾ cup chopped Onion	1 teaspoon Chili Powder
1 No. 2 can Tomatoes	2 tablespoons Lemon Juice
1 cup water	¼ teaspoon Rosemary

Season the fowl with Salt and Pepper, and dredge in Flour. Brown in hot fat. When pieces are brown on both sides, drain off the fat, and add the other ingredients. Cover skillet closely, and place in a 325° F. oven. Bake from 1 hour up to all day, depending on age and disposition of fowl.

Potpourri
of
Seasoning Tips

᪥ Crisp Water Cress, chopped and added at the last moment, will raise the IQ of *Brains* and *Eggs,* a delicious but dull-looking food.

᪥ Poppy Seed add a crunchy, nutty flavor to *Hot Rolls.* Brush tops of unbaked Rolls with melted Butter, and sprinkle generously with the blue Seed.

᪥ Juicy, crisp Raw Onions and Oregano go together, both in *Sandwiches* and the *Salad Bowl.*

᪥ *Cream of Celery Soup* can be quite a surprise when a few Sesame Seed are sprinkled into each serving.

᪥ Water Chestnuts' crisp texture adds interest to *Creamed Chicken.* (Slice the Chestnuts as you would Mushrooms.)

᪥ Traditional *Pound Cake* is so good you may be reluctant to change it, but you'll be happy you did if you add a few Dill Seed to the batter.

᪥ Celery Seed and a little Onion Salt can take the sameness out of *Tuna Fish Salad.*

᪥ *Crisp Sugar Cookies* are better than ever when a few Anise Seed are rolled into the dough. (Children love the licorice flavor of these seed.)

᪥ When toasting Almonds if you brown them too much, don't be dismayed. Burned Almonds give a magnificent crunchiness to *Vanilla Ice Cream.* (Just spoon the crushed nuts on plain.)

᪥ Chop juicy Celery very fine after first "peeling" it with a vegetable peeler, and add to *Fruit Cocktail* that has been drained and mixed with a bit of Mayonnaise. A good quick salad.

⊷§ *Cheese Spreads* of all kinds need the crunchy contrast of seed: Celery, Poppy, Caraway, Sesame, or Dill. (Also these seed make an interesting quick garnish on many other types of *hors-d'oeuvres* spreads.)

⊷§ Sprinkle *Potato Chips* lightly with Curry Powder, and toast them a few minutes. When cool they'll be crisp and savory.

⊷§⥂

FRESH-FLAVORED AND FINE . . .

⊷§ Celery Flakes can save many a *Salad* when the cook finds she's out of fresh Celery. For more flavorful Flakes, place them in a tea strainer, and dunk them in and out of boiling water. Repeat in cold water. Drain well.

⊷§ When making *Peach Preserves,* crack a Peach Seed or two, and add their kernels to the Preserves. They give Preserves a fresh-Peach flavor.

⊷§ On *Sandwiches,* Onion Salt gives a mild but fresh flavor, one that carries no disadvantage of tears or perfumed fingers. (Try Flavor Salt on *Sandwiches,* too—especially *Roast Beef.*)

⊷§ *Canned Soups* have a fine flavor when a little Celery Salt is stirred into them. (This Salt goes with practically *everything.*)

⊷§ *Parsleyed Potatoes* are no trouble at all with Parsley Flakes. Let the Flakes stand in the warm melted Butter or Margarine a few minutes before pouring it over the Potatoes.

⊷§ Sometimes the Chopped Onion in *Meat Loaf* doesn't quite get done. It's easier to use Onion Flakes, and they *always* cook quickly.

⊷§ Have you tried Garlic Salt or Powder in *Shrimp Salad?* Not too much of the Salt, and less of the Powder. Really fresh-flavored and fine.

⋙ Some of the best-flavored short cuts of modern cookery are the Dehydrated Flakes, Powders, and Leaves. In addition to being easier and quicker to use than in their original fresh form, they take up practically no storage space. Cooks most frequently reach for these time-savers to season *Soups, Stews, Sauces, Gravies,* and other foods that have plenty of liquid, for liquid brings out their full fresh flavors.

⋙⋘

SAVORY AND STIMULATING . . .

⋙ *Stuffing for Veal* is better if it carries ½ teaspoon Basil, along with the usual Sage. (*Turtle Soup* must have a bit of Basil in it.)

⋙ *Tamale Pie* is more savory when ¼ teaspoon Cumin Seed is mixed into the cooking Corn Meal Mush.

⋙ Whole Peppercorns will add a more stimulating flavor to *Pot Roast* than ground Pepper.

⋙ If you like *Avocados,* remember that Chili Powder greatly improves their rich blandness. You may want to add the Powder to the *French Dressing* to go over the green slices.

⋙ A whisper of Oregano in *Beef Stew* is wonderful!

⋙ And about those *Avocados:* Some hostesses like to serve them unchilled with their centers filled with heat-hot *French Dressing* made more savory by a bit of Marjoram. Good first course for a winter dinner.

⋙ For a good sauce to go over *Hot Sliced Chicken,* thin a can of Cream of Mushroom Soup with a little Milk and season brightly with ¼ teaspoon Flavor Salt and a pinch of ground Thyme.

⊷ *Salmon Croquettes*—a supper dish almost everyone likes—can be varied interestingly by ¼ teaspoon Marjoram. Another time, try Mace.

⊷ *Spaghetti Sauce* is unusually good when enhanced by ¼ teaspoon Basil.

⊷ *Lamb Stew* needs *something*—like 2 or 3 Whole Allspice.

⊷ That hearty, economical dish that men love, *Braised Oxtails,* will be praised anew when they have been rubbed with Ground Ginger before cooking.

⊷ *Cheese Sauce* needs lots of Dry Mustard, a teaspoon of Mustard to four cups of sauce.

⊷⟊⊷

SWEET AND PUNGENT . . .

⊷ Ornament *Hot Applesauce* with a few Anise Seed before spooning it onto *French Toast.*

⊷ Speaking of Toast, Junior will like the same Seed in his *Milk Toast.*

⊷ Crack three or four tiny Cardamom Seed, and stir them into *Raspberry Preserves.* Let stand one day before using. Good on *Hot Biscuits.* Good as a garnish on *Whipped-Cream-Topped Desserts.*

⊷ After simmering *Corned Beef* until tender, drain, rub with Brown Sugar and a little juice from the Sweet Pickle jar, and stud with hotly-sweet Whole Cloves. Bake 10 minutes to "set" the glaze.

⊷ *Waldorf Salad* is good as is. Better when bedecked with a few crushed Fennel Seed.

⊷ Sweet Vegetables, like *Asparagus* and *Broccoli,* need a speck of Nutmeg's sweet pungency.

◢§ *Lima Beans,* another sweet-flavored vegetable, can be improved by a little Savory.

◢§ Mace's light flavor is just right in little *Cup Cakes* to please the children.

◢§ To give a special aroma to *Fruit Salad Dressing,* blend in a pinch of Apple Pie Spice.

◢§ *Chocolate Fudge* has a more interesting flavor when the candy has ¼ teaspoon Cinnamon beaten into it.

◢§ If Junior won't eat his *Dry Cereal* in the mornings, a few fragrant flecks of Nutmeg may persuade him. (Wonderful on *Grapenuts!*)

◈◈◈

TART AND TANGY . . .

◢§ A Lemon Wedge goes on the side of the *Asparagus Salad Plate.* (Most foods—even sweets—need Lemon's tartness.)

◢§ Turmeric will be more appreciated when better understood: It can go any place Mustard does. See what it can do for the color and the flavor of *Creamed Eggs.*

◢§ *Beef Stew* can be lifted to a higher level by a few Pickle Spice.

◢§ *Rhubarb Sauce's* tartness is softened by a speck of Nutmeg.

◢§ *Sweet Pickles,* even the jar from the store, can be made better by dropping a few Anise Seed into them.

◢§ *French Dressing* becomes monotonous if we don't vary it occasionally. ¼ teaspoon Thyme is an easy variation that's grand on *Green Salads.*

◢§ Dainty green Nasturtium Leaves add an unusual tang to the *Salad Bowl.*

❧ Open a can of ready-seasoned Tomato Sauce, and pour Sauce over browned *Hamburgers* that have a bit of Oregano in them. Cover, and place in 300° F. oven. These make it easy for the hostess to chat without fear of a menu disaster.

❧ Any *Boiled Seafood* can be improved by a few Pickle Spice. (And if you live where Figs grow, also add a Fig Leaf or two—especially to Shrimp.)

❧ When the last Olive is gone, don't pour out the briny juice. It's a perfectly wonderful seasoning for *Stuffed Eggs*.

❧ For an especially refreshing flavor in *Iced Tea,* add a few Mint Leaves to the steeping Tea.

Seasoning Chart

APPETIZERS, CANAPÉS, HORS-D'OEUVRES

AVOCADO DIPS
  Cayenne, Celery Salt, Chili Powder, Curry Powder, Dill Seed, Durkee's
  Famous Dressing, Flavor Salt, Garlic, Lemon Juice, Onion, Paprika,
  Parsley, Tabasco Sauce, Worcestershire Sauce

BUTTER SPREADS
  Anchovy Paste, Basil, Capers, Caraway Seed, Cayenne, Celery Flakes or
  Salt, Chives, Curry Powder, Dill Seed, Flavor Salt, Garlic, Gumbo Filé,
  Lemon Juice, Nasturtiums, Onion, Paprika, Parsley, Poppy Seed, Smoke
  Flavor, Tabasco Sauce, Water Cress, Worcestershire Sauce

CHEESE SPREADS
  Anchovy Paste, Beef Extract, Bitters, Cayenne, Celery Seed, Chives,
  Cognac, Cumin Seed, Curry Powder, Durkee's Famous Dressing, Flavor
  Salt, Horseradish, Nasturtiums, Onion, Paprika, Parsley, Poppy Seed,
  Sage, Smoke Flavor, Tabasco Sauce, Water Cress, Wine, Worcestershire
  Sauce

POTATO CHIPS, TOASTED
  Curry Powder, Garlic Powder or Salt, Onion Powder or Salt

BEVERAGES

ANISETTE
  Anise
BEER
  Nutmeg
CHOCOLATE, HOT
  Cinnamon, Mint
CIDER, MULLED
  Allspice, Cinnamon, Cloves, Nutmeg
COCKTAILS
  Grenadine Sirup, Lemon, Mint, Woodruff
COFFEE
  Anise Seed, Cardamom Seed, Stick Cinnamon, Cognac, Coriander Seed

CRANBERRY JUICE
Ground Cloves, Rue

EGGNOG
Nutmeg, Vanilla

FLIP
Nutmeg

GINGER SOUR
Ginger

HORSE'S NECK
Ginger Ale, Lemon

JUICES AND PUNCH, FRUIT
Balm, Bergamot, Borage, Burnet, Cloves, Grenadine Sirup, Hyssop, Lavender, Lemon, Lemon Verbena, Marjoram, Mint, Rose Geranium, Rose Petals, Woodruff

JUICES, VEGETABLE
Basil, Bay Leaf, Celery Salt, Flavor Salt, Garlic, Lemon, Mace, Marjoram, Onion, Oregano, Rosemary, Rue, Tarragon, Thyme, Worcestershire Sauce

LEMONADE
Balm, Burnet, Lavender, Marjoram, Mint, Woodruff

MAIBOWLE
Woodruff

MILK, HOT
Anise Seed, Fennel Seed, Marigold, Sage, Vanilla

TEA
Balm, Anise Seed, Ginger, Mint, Nasturtium Seed

TEAS, SPICED
Allspice, Cinnamon, Cloves, Lemon, Nutmeg

TEAS, TONIC
Balm, Bergamot, Camomile, Caraway, Catnip, Costmary, Fennel, Horehound, Lovage, Sage, Sassafras, Tansy

TOMATO JUICE
Curry Powder, Mace, Marjoram, Oregano, Worcestershire Sauce

WINE CUPS
Balm, Bergamot, Borage, Lavender, Lemon Verbena, Mint, Rosemary, Woodruff

WINES, MULLED
Cardamom Seed, Stick Cinnamon, Whole Cloves, Mace, Nutmeg

BREADS

BISCUIT
Poultry Seasoning, Rosemary, Sausage Seasoning, Savory, Sesame Seed,
Water Cress

CORN BREAD
Beef Extract, Chicken Fat, Cracklings (Recipe), Onion Flakes, Parsley
(Recipe), Poultry Seasoning, Rosemary

CRUMPETS
Sesame Seed

MUFFINS
Celery Seed, Cinnamon, Nutmeg, Onion

POPOVERS
Mace (Recipe)

ROLLS, PLAIN
Cumin Seed, Fennel Seed (Recipe), Garlic, Lemon (Recipe under Sesame Seed), Onion Flakes, Poppy Seed, Saffron

ROLLS, SWEET
Anise Seed, Cinnamon, Fennel Seed, Lovage, Mincemeat Spice, Pie and
Pudding Spice, Poppy Seed, Saffron

RYE AND OTHER DARK BREADS
Caraway Seed, Dill Seed

SCONES
Sesame Seed

TOAST
Cinnamon, Mayonnaise

WAFFLES
Anise Seed, Apple Pie Spice, Cinnamon

CHEESE DISHES

BALLS, CHEESE
Cayenne, Marjoram, Paprika, Parsley, Tabasco Sauce, Water Cress, Wine,
Worcestershire Sauce

CASSEROLES, RAREBITS, SAUCES
Basil, Cayenne, Celery Salt, Chervil, Chili Powder, Cognac, Fine Herbs,
Flavor Salt, Ginger, Mace, Marjoram, Mushroom Sauce, Dry Mustard,
Onion, Paprika, Pepper, Rue, Sage, Tabasco Sauce (Recipe), Tarragon,
Thyme, Tomato, Wine, Worcestershire Sauce

CHEESE, COTTAGE

Borage, Burnet, Caraway Seed, Celery Salt or Seed, Chervil, Chives, Dill Seed, Garlic, Marjoram, Nasturtium Blossoms and Leaves, Onion, Paprika, Parsley, Pepper, Pimiento, Sage, Tarragon, Water Cress, Worcestershire Sauce

CHEESE, CREAM

Anchovy Paste, Beef Extract, Bitters, Borage, Burnet, Caraway Seed, Celery Salt or Seed, Chervil, Chili Powder, Chives, Cognac, Coriander, Cumin Seed, Dill Seed, Fennel Seed, Garlic, Horseradish (Recipe), Mint, Mustard, Nasturtiums, Onion, Paprika, Parsley, Pimientos, Poppy Seed, Rue, Sage, Sesame Seed, Tabasco Sauce, Water Cress, Wine, Worcestershire Sauce

SOUFFLÉS, CHEESE

Basil, Cayenne, Celery Salt, Chervil, Chili Powder, Ginger, Mace, Marjoram, Mushroom Sauce, Paprika, Tabasco Sauce, Water Cress, Worcestershire Sauce

STRAWS, CHEESE

Cayenne, Marjoram, Tabasco Sauce, Worcestershire Sauce

CHUTNEY, CONSERVES, JELLIES, PICKLES, PRESERVES, RELISHES

APPLE BUTTER

Allspice, Cinnamon, Cloves, Lemon, Vinegar

APPLESAUCE AS A MEAT RELISH

Horseradish

CATSUP

Allspice, Cinnamon, Cloves, Garlic, Onion, Paprika, Red Pepper, Vinegar

CHILI SAUCE

Allspice, Cinnamon, Cloves, Garlic, Onion, Paprika, Red Pepper, Vinegar

CHUTNEY

Celery Seed, Fenugreek, Ginger, Mustard Seed, Turmeric, Vinegar

CRANBERRY RELISH

Cloves, Curry Powder, Lemon, Rue

GRAPE JELLY

Cardamom Seed

JAMS AND PRESERVES
 Allspice, Angelica, Stick Cinnamon, Cloves, Ginger (always in Pear),
 Mace, Nutmeg, Rose Petals, Rosemary

JELLIES
 Costmary, Lavender, Lemon Verbena, Mace, Mint, Rose Geranium,
 Rose Petals (Recipe), Wine

MUSTARD SAUCE
 Various blends of herbs and spices, much Dry Mustard, Turmeric,
 Vinegar. Popular for this purpose are Basil, Horseradish, Lovage, Mar-
 joram, Oregano, Parsley, Rosemary, Sage, Tarragon, Thyme.

PICKLES, DILL
 Dill Seed, Mustard Seed, Peppercorns, Red Pepper, Vinegar

PICKLES, MIXED
 Allspice, Bay Leaf, Caraway Seed, Cassia, Celery Seed, Cloves, Coriander
 Seed, Cumin Seed, Ginger, Mace, Mustard Seed, Nutmeg, Onion,
 Peppercorns, Pickle Spice, Red Pepper, Turmeric, Vinegar

PICKLES, SOUR
 Bay Leaf, Caraway Seed, Celery Seed, Garlic, Mustard Seed, Peppercorns, Pickle Spice, Red Pepper, Tarragon, Vinegar

PICKLES, SWEET
 Allspice, Anise Seed, Cardamom Seed, Celery Seed, Cinnamon, Cloves,
 Coriander Seed, Ginger, Mace, Mustard Seed, Nutmeg, Pickle Spice,
 Vinegar

PINEAPPLE SLICES, BROILED, TO ACCOMPANY MEAT
 Cloves, Curry Powder

RASPBERRY JELLY OR PRESERVES
 Cardamom Seed

STRAWBERRY PRESERVES
 Cardamom Seed

CONFECTIONS

The following Flavorings, Herbs, Spices, and other ingredients listed
are used in a wide variety of confections: Angelica, Anise, Borage
Blossoms (Candied), Caramel, Caraway Seed, Cinnamon (Recipe),
Cloves (Recipe), Coriander Seed, Dill Seed, Fennel Seed, Fenugreek,
Ginger, Horehound, Hyssop, Lemon, Mincemeat Spice (Recipe), Mint,
Poppy Seed, Rose Petals (Candied), Roses Glacé, Sesame Seed, Vanilla,
Violets (Candied)

DESSERTS

CAKES

Apple Upsidedown: Apple Pie Spice; Applesauce: Allspice, Cloves, Cinnamon, Nutmeg; Butter: Allspice, Mace, Nutmeg; Cheese: Lemon, Sesame Seed, Vanilla; Chocolate: Cinnamon, Instant Coffee (for Mocha); Coffee: Anise Seed, Cinnamon, Fennel Seed, Cardamom Seed; Devil's Food: Apple Pie Spice (Recipe); Fruit: Allspice, Angelica, Cinnamon, Cloves, Nutmeg, Mace, Poppy Seed, Pumpkin Pie Spice, Wine; Pineapple Upsidedown: Ginger; Pound: Caraway Seed, Costmary, Dill Seed, Mace, Rose Geranium, Rose Petals or Rose Water; Queen Cakes: Cinnamon (Recipe); Spice: Allspice, Anise, Apple Pie Spice, Cloves, Cinnamon, Ginger, Mace, Nutmeg, Mincemeat Spice (Recipe), Pumpkin Pie Spice; White: Angelica, Instant Coffee, Any Pie or Pudding Spice Blend; Yellow: Mace, Nutmeg

FROSTINGS AND FILLINGS

Apple Pie Spice, Mincemeat Spice, Poppy Seed, Pumpkin Pie Spice, Pie and Pudding Spice, Rose Geranium, Rose Petals

COOKIES

Brownies: Instant Coffee (for Mocha), Cinnamon; Ginger: Ginger; Molasses: Allspice, Cinnamon, Cloves, Nutmeg, Apple Pie Spice, Pie or Pudding Spice, Mincemeat Spice; Pfeffernusse: Cardamom Seed; Refrigerator: Anise Seed (Recipe), Fennel Seed, Ginger (Recipe); Rolled: Anise Seed, Caraway Seed, Dill Seed (Recipe), Horehound, Fennel Seed, Poppy Seed, Sesame Seed, Turmeric; Spice: Allspice, Apple Pie Spice, Cinnamon, Cloves, Nutmeg, Mace, Mincemeat Pie Spice, Pie and Pudding Spice; Springerele: Anise Seed; Sugar: Anise Seed, Coriander Seed, Cumin Seed, Fennel Seed, Horehound, Mint

FRUIT DISHES

Apple Dumplings: Allspice, Apple Pie Spice, Cinnamon, Nutmeg; Apple Rings, Candied: Apple Pie Spice; Apple Strudel: Apple Pie Spice; Apples, Baked: Apple Pie Spice, Cardamom Seed, Cinnamon, Mint (Recipe), Nutmeg, Wine; Apples, Fried: Apple Pie Spice, Nutmeg; Apples, Stewed: Cinnamon, Coriander Seed, Nutmeg; Applesauce: Anise Seed, Apple Pie Spice, Cinnamon, Coriander Seed, Ginger, Mint, Nutmeg, Pumpkin Pie Spice; Bananas and Cream: Nutmeg; Brown Betty: Allspice, Apple Pie Spice, Wine; Cherry Jubilee: Cognac; Fruit Compotes and Cups: Balm, Cognac, Dittany, Grenadine Sirup, Hyssop, Mint, Rose Geranium, Rose Petals, Wine, Woodruff; Fruit, Stewed: Allspice, Apple Pie Spice, Cinnamon, Coriander Seed, Cumin Seed, Cognac,

Lemon, Mace, Wine; Grapefruit, Broiled: Cardamom Seed; Melon Balls: Cardamom Seed, Rose Petals, Wine; Mincemeat: Allspice, Cinnamon, Cloves, Mincemeat Pie Spice, Wine; Peach Jubilee: Cognac; Peaches, Stewed: Cognac, Coriander Seed, Fennel Seed, Ginger, Rose Granium; Pears: Cinnamon, Coriander Seed, Ginger; Prunes: Stick Cinnamon, Coriander Seed, Ginger

GELATINS

Bavarian Cream: Instant Coffee; Coffee: Cardamom Seed; Cranberry Mold: Cloves; Fruit: Hyssop; Plain: Cardamom, Instant Coffee

PIES

Apple: Anise Seed, Apple Pie Spice, Cardamom Seed, Cinnamon, Coriander Seed, Dill Seed; Cherry: Mace; Chess: Lemon, Vinegar (Recipe); Chocolate: Cinnamon, Mace, Mint; Custard: Caramel Sirup, Nutmeg; Fruit: Cumin Seed, Hyssop, Lemon, Mace; Grape: Cardamom Seed (Recipe); Lemon: Nutmeg; Mincemeat: Allspice, Cinnamon, Cloves, Mincemeat Spice; Pastry for Pies: Ginger, Nutmeg, Poppy Seed, Sesame Seed; Peach: Cinnamon; Pecan: Pie and Pudding Spice (Recipe); Pumpkin: Ginger, Pie and Pudding Spice, Pumpkin Pie Spice; Raisin: Cinnamon, Wine; Rhubarb: Nutmeg; Squash: Pie and Pudding Spice; Sweet Potato: Pie and Pudding Spice

PUDDINGS, CUSTARDS, SWEET SOUFFLÉS

Bread: Cinnamon, Coriander Seed, Fennel Seed, Nutmeg, Pie and Pudding Spice, Pumpkin Pie Spice; Chocolate: Cinnamon, Cloves, Mace; Custard: Caramel Sirup, Lemon, Mace, Marigold, Rose Geranium, Rose Petals, Tansy, Vanilla (Recipe); Indian: Ginger; Orange Soufflé: Cayenne; Plum: Allspice, Cinnamon, Cloves, Cognac, Nutmeg, Wine; Rice: Coriander Seed, Fennel Seed, Nutmeg, Pie and Pudding Spice, Pumpkin Pie Spice, Rose Geranium, Rose Petals; Tapioca: Coriander Seed, Ginger

SAUCES AND TOPPINGS

Caramel: Caramel Sirup (Recipe); Cornstarch: Lemon, Mincemeat Spice, Nutmeg (Recipe), Wine; Custard: Instant Coffee, Lemon, Nutmeg, Mace; Grenadine Sirup: Use plain in small quantities, or mixed in other sauces; Honey: Cardamom Seed, Lemon Juice, Poppy Seed, Rose Petals; Whipped Cream: Apple Pie Spice, Instant Coffee, Mace, Nutmeg, Pie and Pudding Spice

SHERBETS AND ICE CREAMS

Baked Alaska: Cognac (Recipe); Ice Cream Base: Caramel Sirup, Cinnamon, Instant Coffee, Lemon, Mint, Rose Geranium, Vanilla

SWEET DOUGHS

Coffee Cake: Cardamom Seed, Cinnamon, Instant Coffee; Danish
Pastries: Cardamom Seed, Coriander Seed; Doughnuts: Cloves, Mace,
Nutmeg, Pie and Pudding Spice; Gingerbread: Coriander Seed, Ginger,
Mace; Sweet Rolls: Anise Seed, Cardamom Seed, Cinnamon, Fennel
Seed, Lovage, Mincemeat Spice, Pie and Pudding Spice, Poppy Seed,
Saffron

EGG DISHES

CASSEROLES, EGG

Allspice, Basil, Cayenne, Celery Flakes or Salt, Chili Powder, Chives,
Chop Suey Sauce, Curry Powder, Dill Seed, Fennel, Fine Herbs, Flavor
Salt, Garlic Salt, Mushroom Sauce, Dry Mustard, Onion Salt, Paprika,
Parsley, Pepper, Pimiento, Roastmeat Seasoning, Rue, Sage, Smoke
Flavor, Tabasco Sauce, Thyme, Tomato, Turmeric, Water Cress, Wine,
Worcestershire Sauce

EGG FOO YUNG SAUCE

Capers (Recipe), Celery, Onion, Pepper, Soy Sauce, Worcestershire
Sauce

EGGS, FRIED OR SCRAMBLED; AND OMELETS

Anchovy Paste, Basil, Celery Salt, Celery Flakes, Chervil, Chili Powder,
Chives, Cognac, Curry Powder, Fine Herbs, Flavor Salt, Marjoram,
Mushroom Sauce, Nutmeg, Oregano, Paprika, Parsley, Poppy Seed,
Savory, Sorrel, Tabasco Sauce, Tansy, Tarragon, Violet Leaves, Worces-
tershire Sauce

EGGS, STUFFED

Anchovy Paste, Celery Salt, Cayenne, Chili Powder, Cumin Seed, Curry
Powder, Durkee's Famous Dressing, Flavor Salt, Lemon, Dry or Pre-
pared Mustard, Paprika, Parsley, Savory, Tabasco Sauce, Tarragon,
Thyme, Turmeric, Vinegar, Worcestershire Sauce

SANDWICHES, BOILED EGG

Anchovy Paste, Celery Salt, Durkee's Famous Dressing, Flavor Salt,
Onion Salt, Paprika, Parsley

SOUFFLÉS, EGG

Cayenne, Celery Salt, Chili Powder, Paprika, Parsley, Tabasco Sauce,
Turmeric, Worcestershire Sauce

FISH AND SHELLFISH

BISQUES
Caraway Seed, Cayenne, Celery Salt, Lemon, Mace, Dry Mustard, Paprika, Parsley, White Pepper

BOUILLABAISSE
Bay Leaf, Cloves, Garlic, Leeks, Lemon, Olive Oil, Onion, Paprika, Parsley, Peppercorns, Saffron, Tomato, Wine

CHOWDERS
Caraway Seed, Cayenne, Chili Powder, Lemon, Lovage, Mace, Marigold, Onion, Paprika, Parsley, Sage, Tarragon, Thyme

CLAM CHOWDER
Onion, Pepper, Pork, Thyme, Tomato

CLAM JUICE
Celery Salt, Lemon, Marjoram, Thyme, Worcestershire Sauce

CLAMS
Caraway Seed, Lemon, Marjoram

COD, BOILED
Allspice, Angelica, Anise Seed, Lemon, Mace, Paprika, Parsley, Shallots

COD FISH CAKES
Cayenne, Celery Salt

COD, SALT
Sage

CRAB
Anise Seed, Cognac, Lemon, Marjoram, Mustard, Oregano, Paprika, Parsley, White Pepper, Rosemary

CRAB FILLING FOR TOMATOES
Anchovy Paste (Recipe)

CROQUETTES
Cayenne, Celery Salt, Mustard, Onion Salt, Paprika, Parsley, White Pepper

FISH BALLS
Cayenne, Thyme

FISH, BAKED
Cloves, Curry Powder, Lemon, Mace, Paprika, Parsley, Marjoram, Sage, Thyme

FISH, BOILED
Allspice, Angelica, Anise, Fennel, Lemon, Mace, Paprika, Parsley, Pickle Spice

FISH, BROILED

Anchovy Paste in Butter Sauce, Curry Powder, Durkee's Famous Dressing, Lemon, Mace, Paprika, Parsley

FISH AND SHELLFISH SAUCES

Capers, Cayenne, Celery Salt, Chervil, Chili Powder, Chives, Coriander, Cumin Seed, Curry Powder, Dill Seed, Fennel, Flavor Salt, Horseradish, Lemon, Mace, Mint, Mirepoix, Mustard, Oregano, Paprika, Parsley, Pimiento, Saffron, Savory (use especially in Horseradish Sauce), Tabasco Sauce, Tarragon, Thyme, Tomato, Turmeric, Vinegar, Water Cress, Worcestershire Sauce

GUMBOS

Filé, Oregano, Smoke Flavor, Thyme

HADDOCK, BOILED

Allspice, Lemon, Mace, Paprika, Parsley, Pickle Spice

HALIBUT, BOILED

Allspice, Angelica, Anise Seed, Basil, Fennel, Lemon, Mace, Paprika, Parsley, Shallots

LOBSTER

Bay Leaf (Recipe), Cayenne, Dill Seed, Lemon, Dry Mustard, Onion, Paprika, Parsley, Pickle Spice, Tarragon

MACKEREL

Basil, Cayenne, Lemon, Mace, Paprika, Parsley

OYSTER STEW

Caraway Seed, Cayenne, Celery Salt, Curry Powder, Mace, Marjoram, Nutmeg, Paprika, Parsley, Thyme

OYSTERS

Cayenne, Chili Powder, Horseradish, Lemon, Mace, Nutmeg, Thyme

RED SNAPPER

Allspice, Lemon, Mace, Parsley

SALMON

Celery Seed, Mace, Marjoram, Tarragon

SEAFOOD, BOILED

Balm, Bay Leaf, Borage, Chervil, Cumin Seed, Dill Seed, Dittany, Fennel, Lemon, Lovage, Mace, Marjoram, Dry Mustard, Onion, Oregano, Paprika, Parsley, Red Pepper, Rosemary, Rue, Saffron, Savory, Sesame Seed, Sorrel, Tabasco Sauce, Tansy, Thyme, Wine, Worcestershire Sauce

SEAFOOD SALADS

Basil, Capers, Cayenne, Fennel, Lemon, Mace, Dry Mustard, Onion, Paprika, Parsley, White Pepper, Pimiento, Worcestershire Sauce

SHRIMP
Anise, Basil, Bay Leaf, Caraway Seed, Cayenne, Chili Powder, Curry Powder, Dill Seed, Fennel, Horseradish, Lemon, Paprika, Parsley, White Pepper, Pickle Spice, Vinegar

TROUT
Marjoram

TUNA FISH
Rue, Tarragon (Recipe), Onion, Celery, Pimiento, Lemon

WHITEFISH
Angelica, Lemon, Mace, Paprika, Parsley, Red Pepper, Shallots

GARNISHES

APPETIZERS
Anchovies, Capers, Caraway Seed, Celery Seed, Chervil, Chives, Dill Seed, Mint, Mushrooms, Nasturtiums, Paprika, Parsley, Pimiento, Poppy Seed, Sesame Seed, Truffles, Water Cress

BEVERAGES
Bergamot, Borage, Lavender, Lemon, Lemon Verbena, Lovage, Mint, Nasturtiums, Rose Petals, Violets

CHEESE AND EGG DISHES
Capers, Celery, Chervil, Chives, Fennel, Paprika, Parsley, Pimientos, Poppy Seed, Truffles

DESSERTS
Angelica, Borage, Candied Ginger, Lavender, Lemon Verbena, Mint, Nasturtiums, Poppy Seed, Rose Geranium, Rose Petals, Sesame Seed, Violets

FISH
Anchovies, Capers, Celery, Chervil, Lemon, Paprika, Parsley, Pimiento, Tarragon, Truffles, Water Cress

MEATS AND MEAT DISHES
Anchovies, Anise Sprigs, Caraway Seed, Celery, Chervil, Chives, Dill Seed, Fennel, Mushrooms, Paprika, Parsley, Pimiento, Tarragon, Truffles, Water Cress

PASTRIES AND BREADS
Anise Seed, Caraway Seed, Dill Seed, Fennel Seed, Poppy Seed, Sesame Seed

POULTRY

Celery, Chervil, Chives, Lemon, Mushrooms, Paprika, Parsley, Pimiento, Poppy Seed, Sesame Seed, Tarragon, Truffles, Water Cress

SALADS

Anchovies, Anise, Capers, Caraway Seed, Celery, Chervil, Chives, Dill, Lemon, Mint, Nasturtiums, Paprika, Parsley, Pimiento, Poppy Seed, Rose Petals, Sesame Seed, Tarragon, Truffles, Violets, Water Cress

SAUCES

Anchovies, Capers, Celery Flakes, Chervil, Chives, Mushrooms, Onion Flakes, Paprika, Parsley, Pimiento, Poppy Seed, Sorrel, Truffles, Water Cress

SOUPS

Caraway Seed, Celery Flakes, Chervil, Chives, Dill Seed, Lemon, Onion Flakes, Paprika, Parsley, Poppy Seed, Water Cress

VEGETABLES

Anise, Caraway Seed, Celery Leaves or Flakes, Chervil, Chives, Dill Seed, Lemon, Mint, Mushrooms, Nasturtiums, Paprika, Parsley, Pimiento, Poppy Seed, Sesame Seed, Truffles, Water Cress

MEATS, SAUCES, STUFFINGS

BEAR

Bay Leaf, Coriander Seed, Cumin Seed, Juniper Berries, Marinade, Marjoram

BEEF, BARBECUED

Cayenne, Chili Powder, Flavor Salt, Garlic, Onion, Tomato, Vinegar, Worcestershire Sauce

BEEF, BOILED

Bay Leaf, Cloves, Dill Seed, Fennel, Horseradish, Lovage, Marinade, Marjoram

BEEF, BRAISED

Bay Leaf, Borage, Chervil, Coriander, Costmary, Fennel, Fine Herbs, Hyssop, Juniper Berries, Lovage, Marigold, Marinade, Marjoram, Mushrooms, Mushroom Sauce, Oregano, Rue, Smoke Flavor, Sorrel, Worcestershire Sauce

BEEF, CORNED

Bay Leaf, Cloves, Horseradish

BEEF DISHES
Bay Leaf, Cardamom Seed, Curry Powder, Fennel, Lovage, Marjoram, Onion, Worcestershire Sauce

BEEF, DRIED
Horseradish (Recipe), Sage

BEEF HASH, CORNED
Horseradish, Marjoram, Onion, Thyme

BEEF PIES
Basil, Bay Leaf, Onion, Tansy, Thyme, Beef Extract, Bouillon Cubes

BEEF, ROAST
Bay Leaf, Cardamom Seed, Catnip, Cloves, Flavor Salt, Lemon, Marinade, Mirepoix, Mushroom Sauce, Mustard, Rosemary, Smoke Flavor (Recipe), Soy Sauce, Thyme, Worcestershire Sauce

BEEF, SPICED ROUND OF
Allspice, Ground Cloves, Red Pepper

BEEF STEW
Bay Leaf, Beef Extract, Bouillon Cubes, Celery Seed, Nutmeg, Onion, Tomato, Peppercorns, Pickle Spice

BRAINS
Cayenne, Marjoram, Paprika, Vinegar, Water Cress, Worcestershire Sauce

CHILI
Beef Extract, Bouillon Cubes, Chili Powder, Cinnamon, Cumin Seed, Garlic, Meat Drippings, Onion, Oregano

CURRIED MEATS
Cardamom Seed, Coriander Seed, Cumin Seed, Fenugreek, Saffron, Turmeric

FRANKFURTERS
Chili Powder, Mustard, Onion, Tomato

GAME
Bay Leaf, Cardamom Seed, Cloves, Cognac, Coriander Seed, Cumin Seed, Hyssop, Juniper Berries, Lemon, Lovage, Marigold, Marinade, Marjoram, Mustard, Oregano, Pickle Spice, Vinegar

GOULASHES
Allspice, Lovage, Onion, Hot Hungarian Paprika, Peppercorns, Tomato, Worcestershire Sauce

GRAVIES
Brown: Allspice, Bay Leaf, Beef Extract, Bouillon Cubes, Caramel Sirup, Chop Suey Sauce, Coriander Seed, Cumin Seed, Dill Seed, Flavor

Salt, Garlic, Juniper Berries, Lovage, Meat Drippings, Mirepoix, Mushroom Sauce, Mushrooms, Onion, Parsley, Rosemary, Savory, Soy Sauce, Tomato, Vinegar, Worcestershire Sauce

Cream: Anise Leaves, Balm, Basil, Beef Extract, Bitters, Bouillon Cubes, Cayenne, Celery Salt, Chili Powder, Durkee's Famous Dressing, Fine Herbs, Flavor Salt, Mace, Mirepoix, Paprika, Parsley, Poultry Seasoning, Red Pepper, Sage, Tabasco Sauce, Worcestershire Sauce

HAM, BOILED

Angelica, Basil, Bay Leaf, Coriander Seed, Juniper Berries, Mustard, Savory

HAM, BAKED

Cinnamon, Cloves, Ginger, Dry Mustard

HAMBURGER

Allspice, Basil, Celery Seed, Curry Powder, Flavor Salt, Garlic, Lemon, Lovage, Nutmeg, Onion, Oregano, Poultry Seasoning, Sage, Savory, Smoke Flavor, Worcestershire Sauce

HASENPFEFFER

Bay Leaf, Coriander Seed, Cumin Seed, Marinade, Onion, Peppercorns, Pickle Spice, Vinegar

HEART

Bay Leaf, Flavor Salt, Pickle Spice

HOGSHEAD CHEESE

Allspice, Bay Leaf, Cayenne, Cloves, Peppercorns, Red Pepper

KIDNEY

Bay Leaf, Caraway Seed, Dill Seed, Curry Powder, Flavor Salt, Oregano, Peppercorns, Shallots

LAMB, BARBECUED

Cayenne, Garlic, Ginger, Juniper Berries, Onion, Tomato, Vinegar

LAMB CHOPS

Curry Powder, Dill Seed, Flavor Salt, Smoke Flavor, Worcestershire Sauce

LAMB, ROAST

Balm, Basil, Caraway Seed, Curry Powder, Chop Suey Sauce, Cinnamon, Fennel, Flavor Salt, Garlic, Juniper Berries, Lemon, Mace, Mirepoix, Mushroom Sauce, Oregano, Rosemary, Smoke Flavor, Soy Sauce (Recipe), Thyme, Worcestershire Sauce

LEAN CUTS OF MEAT

Lardoons

LIVER

Basil, Caraway Seed, Lemon, Marjoram, Savory, Shallots, Truffles

MARINADES

Bay Leaf, Chili Powder, Flavor Salt, Garlic, Juniper Berries, Lemon, Lovage, Mirepoix, Olive Oil, Onion, Peppercorns, Red Pepper, Pickle Spice, Vinegar, Wine

MEAT ASPICS

Allspice, Basil, Bay Leaf, Cayenne, Cinnamon, Garlic, Lovage, Onion, Tarragon, Worcestershire Sauce

MEAT BALLS OR LOAF

Allspice, Beef Extract (Recipe), Cloves, Coriander Seed, Cumin Seed, Ginger, Mace, Marjoram, Oregano, Poultry Seasoning, Rosemary, Sausage Seasoning, Savory, Thyme, Tomato, Worcestershire Sauce

MEAT CROQUETTES OR FRITTERS

Celery Seed, Flavor Salt, Garlic, Mushroom Sauce, Onion, Poultry Seasoning, Red Pepper, Sage, Sesame Seed, Soy Sauce, Thyme, Worcestershire Sauce

MEAT PIES

Bay Leaf, Beef Extract, Bouillon Cubes, Flavor Salt, Garlic, Mushroom Sauce, Mushrooms, Onion, Paprika, Parsley, Poultry Seasoning, Sausage Seasoning, Sesame Seed (in Pastry), Tansy, Worcestershire Sauce

MUTTON

Bay Leaf, Caraway Seed, Coriander Seed, Horseradish, Juniper Berries, Marjoram, Savory, Sorrel

OXTAILS, BRAISED

Bay Leaf, Flavor Salt, Garlic, Oregano

"PAPRIKAS," HUNGARIAN

Hot Hungarian Paprika or a combination of Sweet Spanish Paprika and Cayenne

PORK, BARBECUED

Cayenne, Chili Powder, Flavor Salt, Garlic, Onion, Tomato, Vinegar, Worcestershire Sauce

PORK CHOPS

Cinnamon, Cloves, Dill Seed, Fennel, Flavor Salt, Ginger, Horseradish, Lemon, Oregano, Poultry Seasoning, Sage (Recipe), Smoke Flavor, Soy Sauce, Thyme

PORK, ROAST

Allspice, Basil, Caraway Seed, Cardamom Seed, Catnip, Cloves, Coriander Seed, Fennel, Flavor Salt, Horseradish, Lemon, Marjoram, Oregano, Mushroom Sauce, Mustard, Poultry Seasoning, Rosemary, Rue, Sage, Sausage Seasoning, Smoke Flavor, Soy Sauce, Thyme

POT ROASTS

Allspice, Bay Leaf, Beef Extract, Bouillon Cubes, Flavor Salt, Ginger, Hyssop, Lemon, Marigold, Mirepoix, Mushroom Sauce, Peppercorns, Worcestershire Sauce

RABBIT

Basil, Bay Leaf, Cumin Seed, Flavor Salt, Hyssop, Juniper Berries, Marinade, Rosemary, Savory, Shallots, Tarragon, Thyme, Vinegar, Wine

RAGOUTS AND STEWS

Allspice, Anise Leaves, Balm, Bay Leaf, Beef Extract, Bouillon Cubes, Borage, Bouquet Garni, Caramel, Caraway Seed, Catnip, Celery Seed, Chervil, Chop Suey Sauce, Cinnamon, Cloves, Coriander Seed, Cumin Seed, Flavor Salt, Garlic, Hyssop, Juniper Berries, Lovage, Marjoram, Meat Drippings, Mirepoix, Mushroom Sauce, Onion, Oregano, Peppercorns, Rosemary, Savory, Shallots, Soy Sauce, Tansy (in Lamb Stew especially), Thyme (Beef), Tomato, Vinegar, Wine, Worcestershire Sauce

SAUCES

Barbecue: Allspice, Cayenne, Chili Powder, Coriander Seed, Flavor Salt, Garlic, Dry Mustard, Onion, Paprika, Pickle Spice, Red Pepper, Smoke Flavor, Tabasco Sauce, Tomato (Recipe), Vinegar, Worcestershire Sauce
Butter: Anchovy Paste, Cayenne, Celery Salt, Chives, Coriander Seed, Fine Herbs, Flavor Salt, Garlic, Horehound, Lemon, Lovage, Onion, Oregano, Paprika, Parsley, Rosemary, Shallots, Worcestershire Sauce
Horseradish: Savory, Vinegar, Wine, Lemon, Flavor Salt
Lamb or Veal: Mint
Spaghetti: Allspice, Basil, Beef Extract, Bouillon Cubes, Cayenne, Chili Powder, Flavor Salt, Garlic, Mushrooms, Onion, Olive Oil, Oregano, Parsley, Tomato, Wine, Worcestershire Sauce
Tomato: Allspice, Basil, Bay Leaf, Cayenne, Flavor Salt, Garlic, Lovage, Marjoram, Mirepoix, Mushroom Sauce, Onion, Olive Oil, Oregano, Parsley, Red Pepper, Wine, Worcestershire Sauce

SAUERBRATEN

Bay Leaf, Flavor Salt, Garlic, Marinade, Onion, Peppercorns, Pickle Spice, Pork, Red Pepper, Vinegar

SAUSAGE

Anise, Bay Leaf, Cardamom Seed, Cloves, Coriander Seed, Cumin Seed, Mace, Marjoram, Mustard, Red Pepper, Sage, Sausage Seasoning, Savory

SPARERIBS

Bay Leaf, Flavor Salt, Chili Powder, Garlic, Mustard, Smoke Flavor, Paprika, Soy Sauce, Worcestershire Sauce

SPICED MEATS

Bay Leaf, Cloves, Coriander Seed, Cumin Seed, Flavor Salt, Garlic, Onion, Parsley, Red Pepper, Peppercorns, Pickle Spice, Vinegar

STEAKS

Allspice, Anchovy Paste, Balm, Basil, Cardamom Seed, Cognac, Durkee's Famous Dressing, Fine Herbs, Garlic, Ginger, Lemon, Mushroom Sauce or Mushrooms, Mustard, Olive Oil, Oregano (Recipe), Shallots, Smoke Flavor, Soy Sauce, Tarragon, Wine

STUFFINGS

Basil, Chervil, Chili Powder, Cloves, Coriander Seed (especially for Game), Flavor Salt, Juniper Berries, Mace, Marjoram, Onion, Oregano, Parsley, Pepper, Rosemary, Sage, Savory, Tansy, Thyme

SWEETBREADS

Cayenne, Flavor Salt, Mace, Onion, Oregano, Paprika, Parsley, White Pepper

TONGUE

Bay Leaf, Cloves, Flavor Salt, Onion, Parsley, Pickle Spice, Vinegar

VEAL

Basil, Bay Leaf, Curry Powder, Dill Seed, Flavor Salt, Ginger, Mace, Marjoram, Mushroom Sauce, Oregano, Poultry Seasoning, Rosemary, Sage, Sausage Seasoning, Shallots, Smoke Flavor, Tarragon, Thyme

VENISON

Basil, Bay Leaf, Cloves, Coriander Seed, Cumin Seed, Costmary, Hyssop, Juniper Berries, Red Pepper, Marinade, Vinegar, Wine

MISCELLANEOUS

POMANDERS (SPICE BALLS)

Whole Cloves (Recipe)

PASTE DISHES

See Vegetables

POULTRY AND STUFFINGS

CHICKEN, BAKED OR ROASTED
Basil, Bay Leaf, Chervil, Costmary, Cumin Seed, Flavor Salt, Garlic (Recipe), Ginger, Lemon, Marjoram, Oregano, Paprika (Recipe), Rosemary, Sage, Thyme

CHICKEN, BROILED
Chervil, Lemon, Marjoram, Rosemary, Sesame Seed, Tarragon, Thyme, Truffles, Wine

CHICKEN, CREAMED
Cayenne, Cognac, Curry Powder, Dill Seed, Ginger, Marinade, Mustard, Nutmeg, Paprika, Parsley, White Pepper, Pimiento, Saffron, Sesame Seed (in Pastry), Shallots, Tabasco Sauce, Turmeric, Wine, Worcestershire Sauce

CHICKEN, STEWED
Bay Leaf, Cloves, Coriander Seed, Cumin Seed, Flavor Salt, Ginger, Marjoram, Mustard, Onion, Paprika, Parsley, White Pepper, Rosemary, Saffron (Recipe), Savory, Shallots, Thyme, Turmeric, Worcestershire Sauce

CROQUETTES
Cayenne, Marjoram, Poultry Seasoning, Rosemary, Sage, Savory, Sesame Seed, Thyme

DUCK
Basil, Bay Leaf, Costmary, Juniper Berries, Marinade, Marjoram, Onion, Oregano, Pepper, Roastmeat Seasoning (excellent on Wild Duck), Sage, Shallots, Tarragon, Truffles (Roast Domestic Duck)

GOOSE
Basil, Bay Leaf, Ginger, Juniper Berries, Marinade, Marjoram, Onion, Paprika, Parsley, Rosemary, Sage, Tarragon, Thyme, Wine

GROUSE
Basil, Bay Leaf, Juniper Berries, Marinade, Marjoram, Onion, Parsley, Poultry Seasoning, Rosemary, Thyme

PHEASANT
Basil, Bay Leaf, Juniper Berries, Marinade, Marjoram, Onion, Rosemary, Sage, Thyme

POULTRY SALADS
Basil, Cayenne, Celery Salt, Cumin Seed, Flavor Salt, Marinade, Marjoram, Onion, Paprika, Parsley, White Pepper, Rosemary, Thyme

QUAIL
Marjoram, Parsley, Rosemary, Thyme

SAUCES

Barbecue: Cayenne, Chili Pepper, Flavor Salt, Garlic, Onion, Smoke Flavor, Tomato (Recipe), Vinegar, Worcestershire Sauce

Butter: Celery Salt, Chervil, Flavor Salt, Garlic, Lemon, Marjoram, Mushrooms, Onion, Paprika, Parsley, Rosemary, Sesame Seed, Tarragon, Thyme, Truffles, Wine

SQUABS

Celery Salt, Chervil, Marjoram, Onion, Paprika, Parsley, Rosemary, Tarragon, Thyme

STUFFINGS

Balm, Celery, Chervil, Marjoram, Onion, Paprika, Parsley, Poultry Seasoning, Rosemary, Sage, Thyme

TURKEY

Marjoram, Onion, Parsley, Rosemary, Savory, Thyme

SALADS

AVOCADO

Water Cress (Recipe)

CELERY, STUFFED

Bitters, Cayenne, Paprika, Parsley, Pimiento, Water Cress

CHEESE, COTTAGE

Basil, Caraway Seed, Celery Salt, Dill Seed, Dittany, Fennel Seed, Marjoram, Onion, Paprika, Parsley, Pimiento, Rue, Sage, Tarragon, Thyme, Water Cress

CHEESE, CREAM

Anchovy Paste, Basil, Bitters, Cayenne, Celery Seed, Chives, Cognac, Cumin Seed, Curry Powder, Flavor Salt, Horseradish, Lemon, Mace, Nasturtiums, Onion, Paprika, Parsley, Pimiento, Poppy Seed, Rose Petals, Sage, Tabasco Sauce, Water Cress, Wine, Worcestershire Sauce.

CHICKEN

Basil, Cayenne, Celery Salt, Cumin Seed, Marinade, Marjoram, Onion, Paprika, Parsley, White Pepper, Rosemary, Thyme

COLE SLAW

Caraway Seed, Celery Seed, Dill Seed, Durkee's Famous Dressing, Fennel Seed, Lemon, Mint, Mustard, Onion, Parsley, Savory, Vinegar, Water Cress

FRUIT

Angelica, Anise Seed, Balm, Celery, Curry Powder, Dittany, Fennel Seed, Grenadine Sirup, Lemon, Marjoram, Mint, Mustard, Rosemary, Water Chestnuts, Water Cress, Wine

GREEN

Anise Leaves, Balm, Basil, Borage, Burnet, Catnip, Celery Leaves, Chervil, Chives, Coriander, Dill, Fennel, Fine Herbs, Flavor Salt, Leeks, Lemon, Lovage, Marjoram, Mint, Nasturtiums, Olive Oil, Onion, Parsley, Purslane, Rue, Savory, Sorrel, Tansy, Thyme, Vinegar, Violet Leaves, Water Cress

KIDNEY BEAN

Celery Salt, Chili Powder, Onion, Pepper, Savory (Recipe)

LOBSTER

Cayenne, Horseradish, Lemon, Mustard, Onion, Paprika, Parsley, Tarragon

MACARONI

Basil, Cayenne, Dill Seed, Flavor Salt, Mace, Onion, Parsley, Tabasco Sauce, Pimiento, Water Cress, Worcestershire Sauce

MEAT

Basil, Cayenne, Celery, Curry Powder, Flavor Salt, Garlic, Lemon, Marjoram, Onion, Rosemary, Thyme, Tomato, Worcestershire Sauce

PEAR

Ginger

POTATO

Borage, Caraway Seed, Celery and Celery Seed, Dill Seed, Durkee's Famous Dressing, Mustard, Onion, Parsley, Pimiento, Savory, Vinegar

SHRIMP

Basil, Cayenne, Celery and Celery Salt, Flavor Salt, Garlic, Horseradish, Lemon, Marinade, Mustard, Paprika, Parsley, Tarragon, Wine, Worcestershire Sauce

TOMATO

Basil, Bay Leaf, Borage, Flavor Salt, Garlic, Lemon, Olive Oil, Onion, Oregano, Parsley, Sage, Savory, Tarragon, Thyme, Water Cress

TUNA

Celery, Cayenne, Flavor Salt, Lemon, Onion, Parsley, Rue, Tarragon (Recipe), White Pepper

VEGETABLE

Anise, Basil, Burnet, Caraway Seed, Celery, Dill Seed, Fennel, Fine Herbs, Flavor Salt, Garlic, Hyssop, Leeks, Lemon, Marjoram, Olive Oil,

Onion, Oregano, Paprika, Parsley, Poppy Seed, Rue, Thyme, Turmeric,
Wine

WALDORF

Anise Seed, Celery, Fennel Seed, Lemon

SALAD DRESSINGS

CELERY SEED

Add a generous portion of Celery Seed to Basic French Dressing

COOKED

Celery Salt, Lemon, Mustard, Paprika, Lemon, Vinegar, Wine (Also
add other Herbs or Spices according to the basic ingredient of salad.)

FRENCH

Anchovy Paste, Basil, Capers, Celery Salt, Chives, Coriander Seed, Curry
Powder, Flavor Salt, Garlic, Ginger, Grenadine Sirup, Lemon, Dry
Mustard, Olive Oil, Onion, Oregano, Paprika, Parsley, Pearl Onions,
Sage, Thyme, Tomato, Vinegar, Water Cress, Worcestershire Sauce

FRUIT

Allspice, Anise Seed, Cardamom Seed, Fennel Seed, Ginger, Lemon,
Mace, Mustard, Nutmeg, Wine

HONEY, WHIPPED

(For Fruit or Melon Salads) Cardamom Seed, Ginger, Grenadine Sirup
(Recipe), Lemon, Mace, Mint, Nutmeg, Wine

MAYONNAISE

Capers, Celery Salt, Chives, Ginger, Lemon, Dry Mustard, Olive Oil,
Turmeric (Recipe), Vinegar, Wine

SOUR CREAM

Chives, Dill Seed, Horseradish, Lemon, Onion Salt, Paprika, Parsley,
Tarragon, Vinegar

SOUPS

BEAN

Balm, Bay Leaf, Celery Salt, Coriander Seed, Cloves, Cumin Seed, Dill
Seed, Fennel, Flavor Salt, Garlic, Ginger, Lemon, Mint, Mustard, Onion,
Oregano, Parsley, Pork, Savory, Tabasco Sauce, Thyme

BEEF

Allspice, Bay Leaf, Bouillon Cubes, Beef Extract, Cloves, Cumin Seed, Fennel, Flavor Salt, Garlic, Marjoram, Nutmeg, Onion, Oregano, Pepper, Worcestershire Sauce

BISQUES

Caraway Seed, Cayenne, Celery Salt, Lemon, Mace, Dry Mustard, Paprika, Parsley, White Pepper

BLACK BEAN

Garlic, Lemon, Nutmeg, Pie and Pudding Spice, Smoke Flavor, Tabasco Sauce

BORSCHT

Cloves, Dill Seed, Lemon, Oregano, Parsley, Thyme

BOUILLABAISSE

Bay Leaf, Cloves, Garlic, Leeks, Lemon, Olive Oil, Onion, Paprika, Parsley, Peppercorns, Saffron, Tomato, Wine

BROTH

Beef Extract, Bouillon Cubes, Hyssop, Lemon, Mace, Onion, Pickle Spice

CHICKEN

Mace, Marigold, Marjoram, Nutmeg, Onion, Parsley, Rosemary, Saffron, Sesame Seed

CLAM CHOWDER

Onion, Pepper, Pork, Thyme, Tomato

CANNED SOUPS

Flavor Salt, Lemon, Sage, Wine

CONSOMMÉ

Allspice, Cloves, Curry Powder, Flavor Salt, Hyssop, Lemon, Mace, Nutmeg, Onions, Parsley, Sage, Thyme

CORN SOUP

Cinnamon, Chili Powder, Paprika, Parsley

CREAM SOUPS

Bitters, Borage, Caraway Seed, Cayenne, Celery Flakes, Dill Seed, Lemon, Mace, Nutmeg, Paprika, Parsley, Sesame Seed, Water Cress, Wine

FISH CHOWDERS AND SOUPS

Bay Leaf, Caraway Seed, Cayenne, Celery, Chili Powder, Dill Seed, Fennel, Lemon, Lovage, Mace, Marigold, Onion, Oregano, Paprika, Parsley, Pork, Poultry Seasoning, Sage, Tarragon, Thyme

GUMBOS

Bay Leaf, Butter, Celery, Filé, Garlic, Lemon, Onion, Paprika, Parsley, Pork (Bacon), Smoke Flavor, Thyme, Tomato

LENTIL SOUP

Borage, Coriander Seed, Cumin Seed, Fennel Seed, Savory, Tomato, Vinegar, Wine

MADRILENE

Bay Leaf, Beef Extract, Bouillon Cubes, Celery, Marjoram, Onion, Peppercorns, Tarragon, Tomato, Vinegar

MINESTRONE

Basil, Oregano, Water Cress

MUSHROOM SOUP

Bitters, Burnet, Celery Salt, Curry Powder, Flavor Salt, Mace, Parsley, Tarragon

ONION SOUP

Basil, Caraway Seed, Cloves, Ginger, Marjoram, Mustard, Oregano, Paprika, Parsley, Poppy Seed, Poultry Seasoning, Sage, Sausage Seasoning

OXTAIL SOUP

Basil, Bay Leaf, Beef Extract, Bouillon Cubes, Garlic, Mirepoix, Onions, Parsley

OYSTER STEW

Caraway Seed, Cayenne, Celery Salt, Curry Powder, Mace, Marjoram, Nutmeg, Paprika, Parsley, Thyme

POTATO SOUP

Basil, Bay Leaf, Chives, Cloves, Dill Seed, Fennel, Ginger, Mace, Mirepoix, Onions, Parsley, Rosemary, Rue, Sage, Sesame Seed, Thyme

SPLIT PEA SOUP

Allspice, Coriander Seed, Lemon, Mint, Nutmeg, Rosemary, Savory, Smoke Flavor, Thyme

TOMATO SOUP

Allspice, Basil, Bay Leaf, Borage, Celery Salt, Chili Powder, Cloves, Curry Powder, Dill Seed, Garlic, Lemon, Mace, Marjoram, Onion, Oregano, Parsley, Sage, Savory, Tarragon, Thyme

TURTLE SOUP

Basil, Lemon, Marjoram, Rosemary, Tarragon

VEGETABLE SOUP

Anise, Basil, Bay Leaf, Beef Extract, Bouillon Cubes, Celery, Fennel, Garlic, Mirepoix, Onion, Parsley, Purslane, Savory, Thyme, Tomato

VICHYSSOISE

Chives, Leeks, Water Cress

VEGETABLES

ARTICHOKES
Bay Leaf, Fennel, Lemon, Olive Oil, Tarragon, Vinegar

ASPARAGUS
Bay Leaf, Caraway Seed, Durkee's Famous Dressing (Recipe), Fennel, Lemon, Marjoram, Olive Oil, Savory, Tarragon

BEANS, BAKED
Allspice, Ginger, Dry Mustard, Onion, Smoke Flavor

BEANS, DRIED
Bay Leaf, Cumin Seed, Pork, Red Pepper, Savory, Tabasco Sauce

BEANS, GREEN
Basil, Bay Leaf, Borage, Cayenne, Whole Cloves, Dill Seed, Fennel, Garlic, Lemon, Marjoram, Mint, Nutmeg, Olive Oil, Onion, Rosemary, Sage, Savory, Tabasco Sauce, Thyme (Recipe)

BEANS, KIDNEY
Bay Leaf, Chili Powder, Onion, Savory

BEANS, LIMA (GREEN)
Basil, Cayenne, Celery Salt, Chives, Fennel, Marjoram, Mustard, Olive Oil, Onion, Savory

BEETS
Bay Leaf, Caraway Seed, Cloves, Dill Seed, Flavor Salt, Lemon, Mustard, Pickle Spice, Tarragon, Vinegar

BROCCOLI
Durkee's Famous Dressing, Garlic, Lemon, Marjoram, Nutmeg, Olive Oil, Oregano, Pickle Spice, Tarragon, Thyme

BRUSSELS SPROUTS
Marjoram, Nutmeg, Olive Oil, Sage, Savory

CABBAGE, GREEN
Borage, Caraway Seed, Celery Seed, Curry Powder, Dill Seed, Fennel, Lemon, Oregano, Paprika, Pickle Spice, Pork, Sage, Savory, Sorrel, Tabasco Sauce, Tarragon, Vinegar

CABBAGE, RED
Allspice, Caraway Seed, Cloves, Cumin Seed, Lemon, Pickle Spice, Savory, Vinegar, Red Pepper

CARROTS
Allspice, Basil, Bay Leaf, Chervil, Chili Powder, Dill Seed, Ginger, Mace, Marjoram, Mint, Olive Oil, Parsley, Poppy Seed (Recipe), Thyme

CAULIFLOWER

Basil, Borage, Caraway Seed, Cayenne, Celery Seed, Dill Seed, Ginger, Mace, Nutmeg, Paprika, Parsley, Poppy Seed, Rosemary, Savory, Tarragon

CELERY

Chili Pepper, Chives, Paprika, Parsley, Tarragon

COLLARDS

Cayenne, Lemon, Nutmeg, Olive Oil, Pork, Purslane, Tabasco Sauce, Tarragon, Vinegar

CORN

Cayenne, Chili Powder, Paprika, Onion, Parsley, Roastmeat Seasoning (Recipe)

CRUMB TOPPINGS FOR VEGETABLE CASSEROLES

Flavor Salt, Olive Oil, Sesame Seed

CUCUMBERS

Basil, Borage, Burnet, Chives, Dill Seed, Lemon, Olive Oil, Onion, Vinegar

EGGPLANT

Allspice, Basil, Bay Leaf, Chili Powder, Fennel, Marjoram, Olive Oil, Oregano, Rosemary, Sage, Savory, Thyme

GREENS, COOKED

Fresh Angelica, Borage, Burnet, Cayenne, Lemon, Nutmeg, Olive Oil, Pork, Purslane, Tabasco Sauce, Tarragon, Vinegar, Water Cress

GRITS

Beef Extract, Bouillon Cubes, Chili Powder, Poultry Seasoning

GUMBOS

Bay Leaf, Butter, Celery, Filé, Garlic, Lemon, Onion, Paprika, Parsley, Pork (Bacon), Smoke Flavor, Thyme, Tomato

KALE

Cayenne, Lemon, Nutmeg, Olive Oil, Pork, Purslane, Tabasco Sauce, Tarragon, Vinegar

LEEKS

Chicken Stock, Olive Oil, Oregano

LENTILS

Bay Leaf, Borage, Butter, Cloves, Coriander, Cumin Seed, Fennel, Nutmeg, Onion, Pork, Paprika, Parsley, Savory, Tomato, Vinegar, Wine

MUSHROOMS

Marjoram, Nutmeg, Olive Oil, Paprika, Parsley, Rue, Tarragon, Vinegar

Mustard Greens

Cayenne, Lemon, Olive Oil, Pork, Purslane, Tabasco Sauce, Tarragon, Vinegar

Onions

Basil, Caraway, Celery Seed, Cloves, Ginger, Marjoram, Mustard, Oregano, Paprika, Parsley, Poppy Seed, Poultry Seasoning, Sage, Sausage Seasoning (Recipe), Thyme

Paste Dishes

Corn Meal Mush: Chili Powder, Parsley, Poultry Seasoning, Rosemary; Dumplings: Marjoram, Parsley, Poultry Seasoning; Macaroni: Basil, Cayenne, Dill Seed, Mace, Mustard, Onion, Parsley, Tabasco Sauce, Pimiento, Worcestershire Sauce; Noodles: Basil, Caraway Seed, Olive Oil, Parsley, Poppy Seed, Sesame Seed, Water Cress; Pizza Pie: Basil, Oregano, or a combination of Parsley, Rosemary, Marjoram, and Thyme; Polenta: Coriander, Paprika, Parsley, Red Pepper; Ravioli: Allspice, Cayenne, Parsley, Tabasco Sauce; Spaghetti: Allspice, Basil, Beef Extract, Bouillon Cubes, Cayenne, Chili Powder, Garlic, Nutmeg, Onion, Oregano, Parsley, Worcestershire Sauce; Tamale Pie: Chili Powder, Cumin Seed, Oregano; Tamales, Hot: Cayenne, Chili Powder, Cumin Seed

Peas, Dried

Bay Leaf, Coriander, Cumin Seed, Oregano, Pork, Savory, Tabasco Sauce

Peas, Green

Basil, Borage, Chervil, Chili Powder, Cinnamon, Marjoram, Mint, Mushrooms, Olive Oil, Oregano, Savory, Tarragon, Thyme

Peppers, Green

Basil, Chili Pepper, Chives (Recipe), Marjoram, Olive Oil

Poke Greens

Cayenne, Lemon, Olive Oil, Pork (Bacon Drippings), Purslane, Tabasco Sauce, Vinegar

Potatoes

Basil, Bay Leaf, Borage, Caraway Seed, Chives, Dill Seed, Durkee's Famous Dressing, Marjoram, Mayonnaise, Mint, Onion, Oregano, Paprika, Parsley, Rosemary, Rue, Sage, Sesame Seed, Thyme, Vinegar

Rice

Basil, Bay Leaf, Chili Powder, Coriander Seed, Cumin Seed, Curry Powder, Paprika, Parsley, Saffron, Savory, Sesame Seed, Tomato, Turmeric

SAUERKRAUT

Caraway Seed, Coriander, Cumin Seed, Dill Seed, Fennel, Juniper Berries, Savory

SPINACH

Basil, Borage, Cayenne, Chervil, Cinnamon, Garlic, Lemon, Mace, Marjoram, Mint, Nutmeg, Olive Oil, Oregano, Pickle Spice, Rosemary, Sorrel, Tabasco Sauce, Tarragon, Thyme, Vinegar

SQUASH

Basil, Cayenne, Cinnamon, Dill Seed, Fennel, Olive Oil, Oregano, Savory

SUCCOTASH

Mace, Mustard, Nutmeg

SWEET POTATOES

Cinnamon, Cloves, Nutmeg, Poppy Seed, Pie and Pudding Spice

SWISS CHARD

Lemon, Olive Oil, Onion, Rosemary

TOMATOES

Allspice, Basil, Bay Leaf, Borage, Cayenne, Chili Powder, Cloves, Curry Powder (on Broiled Tomatoes), Dill Seed, Garlic, Lemon, Mace, Marjoram, Olive Oil, Onion, Oregano, Sage, Savory, Tarragon, Thyme

TURNIP GREENS

Cayenne, Lemon, Nutmeg, Olive Oil, Pork, Savory, Tabasco Sauce

TURNIPS

Basil, Caraway Seed, Cayenne, Dill Seed, Fennel, Pork, Rosemary, Sage, Tabasco Sauce, Vinegar

VEGETABLE FRITTERS

Celery, Flavor Salt, Onion, Poultry Seasoning, Sausage Seasoning, Soy Sauce, Thyme, Tomato

VEGETABLE JUICES

Basil, Bay Leaf, Celery Salt, Curry Powder, Flavor Salt, Garlic Salt, Lemon, Mace, Marjoram, Onion, Oregano, Rosemary, Rue, Tarragon, Thyme, Worcestershire Sauce

VEGETABLE SALADS

Anise, Basil, Burnet, Caraway Seed, Celery, Dill Seed, Fennel, Fine Herbs, Flavor Salt, Garlic, Hyssop, Leeks, Lemon, Marjoram, Olive Oil, Onion, Oregano, Paprika, Parsley, Poppy Seed, Rue, Tarragon Thyme, Turmeric, Wine

VEGETABLE SAUCES

When seasoned with any appropriate condiment, herb, spice, etc. (as shown by this chart), any of the following makes a tasty base for a

Vegetable Sauce: Beef Extract, Bouillon Cubes, Butter, Chicken Fat or Stock, Cooking Water from the Vegetables themselves, Cream of Mushroom or Tomato Soup, Mirepoix, Olive Oil

ZUCCHINI

Basil, Mace, Marjoram

VINEGARS, AROMATIC

Flavored Vinegars, which may be prepared from almost any Herb or Spice, are especially prized for use in salad dressings, sauces, soups, stews, etc. Especially popular for flavoring Vinegars are: Allspice, Balm, Basil, Bay Leaf, Borage, Burnet, Caraway Seed, Celery Seed, Chives, Cinnamon, Cloves, Coriander Seed, Curry Powder, Dill Seed or Plant, Fennel, Garlic, Horseradish, Mace, Marjoram, Mint, Mustard Seed, Nasturtiums, Onion, Peppercorns, Rose Geranium, Rose Petals, Rosemary, Rue, Shallots, Sorrel, Tarragon, Thyme, Wood Violets.